The Surrey Hills
A DOG WALKER'S GUIDE

David and Hilary Staines

COUNTRYSIDE BOOKS
NEWBURY BERKSHIRE

First published 2018
© David and Hilary Staines 2018

Reprinted 2021, 2022

All rights reserved. No part of this publication may be reproduced, stored in a retrieval system, or transmitted by any means, electronic, mechanical, photocopying, recording or otherwise, without the prior written permission of the copyright holder and publishers.

Countryside Books
3 Catherine Road
Newbury, Berkshire

To view our complete range of books
please visit us at
www.countrysidebooks.co.uk

ISBN 978 1 84674 353 5

Photographs by David Staines

The cover photograph shows the North Downs Way

Designed by Peter Davies

Produced by The Letterworks Ltd., Reading
Typeset by KT Designs, St Helens
Printed by The Holywell Press, Oxford

Contents

Area map 4
Introduction 5
🐾 Advice for Dog Walkers 7

Walk

1	Abinger Hammer & Friday Street *(4.5 miles / 7.2 km or 5.5 miles / 8.9 km)*	9
2	Alfold *(6 miles / 9.7 km)*	14
3	Banstead Woods *(2.5 miles / 4 km)*	19
4	Box Hill *(4.5 miles / 7.2 km)*	23
5	Chinthurst Hill *(1.5 miles / 2.4 km)*	28
6	Devil's Punch Bowl *(2.5 miles / 4 km)*	32
7	Farnham *(2 miles / 4 km)*	36
8	Newlands Corner & St Martha's Hill *(4 miles / 6.4 km)*	40
9	Holmbury Hill *(2.5 miles / 4 km)*	44
10	Leith Hill *(2.5 miles / 4 km)*	48
11	Limpsfield Chart *(2.5 miles / 4 km)*	52
12	Loseley Park *(4 miles / 6.4 km)*	57
13	Polesden Lacey *(4.5 miles / 7.2 km)*	61
14	Ranmore *(2.5 miles / 4 km)*	66
15	Reigate Fort & Gatton Park *(3 miles / 4.8 km)*	70
16	Shamley Green *(5 miles / 8 km or 8 miles / 12.8 km)*	74
17	Tatsfield *(2.5 miles / 4 km)*	79
18	Titsey *(4 miles / 6.4 km)*	83
19	Waverley Abbey *(3.5 miles / 5.6 km)*	87
20	Woldingham *(3 miles / 4.8 km)*	92

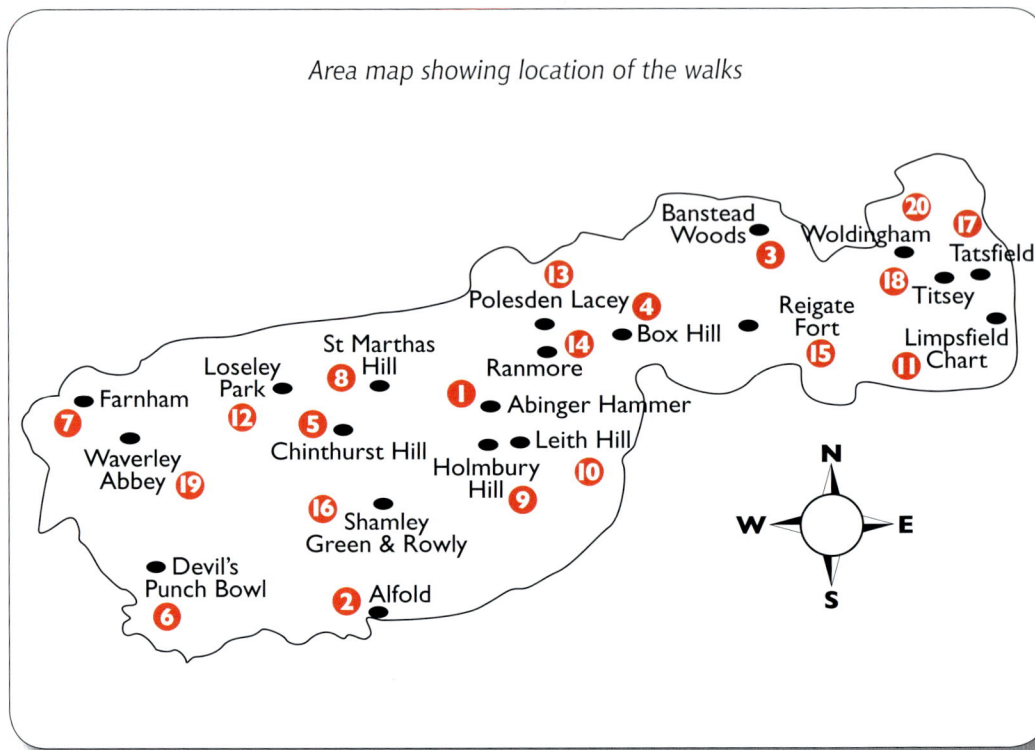

Area map showing location of the walks

PUBLISHER'S NOTE

We hope that you obtain considerable enjoyment from this book; great care has been taken in its preparation. Although at the time of publication all routes followed public rights of way or permitted paths, diversion orders can be made and permissions withdrawn.

We cannot, of course, be held responsible for such diversion orders and any inaccuracies in the text which result from these or any other changes to the routes nor any damage which might result from walkers trespassing on private property. We are anxious though that all details covering the walks are kept up to date and would therefore welcome information from readers which would be relevant to future editions.

The simple sketch maps that accompany the walks in this book are based on notes made by the author whilst checking out the routes on the ground. They are designed to show you how to reach the start, to point out the main features of the overall circuit and they contain a progression of numbers that relate to the paragraphs of the text.

However, for the benefit of a proper map, we do recommend that you purchase the relevant Ordnance Survey sheet covering your walk. The Ordnance Survey maps are widely available, especially through booksellers and local newsagents.

INTRODUCTION

Welcome to this dog walker's guide to the Surrey Hills. The hills stretch from the county border with Kent almost to Hampshire. The 163 square miles were officially designated an Area of Outstanding Natural Beauty in 1958 – meaning it has equal landscape status and protection as a National Park – and covers one quarter of the county of Surrey.

Many of the most famous and popular beauty spots in Southern England are here, including Leith Hill, Box Hill and the Devil's Punch Bowl. There are extensive footpaths and tracks including the famous North Downs Way, Greensand Way and the ancient Pilgrims' Way. With many open commons and rolling hillsides dotted with rural pubs, market towns and villages, rich in wildlife and woodland, it easily provides some of the best walking in England.

It's a long established place to visit to enjoy fresh country air with outstanding scenery and, of course, what better companion to enjoy all this with than your dog? You are sure to be delighted with its variety and beauty, and your 'faithful friend' will be enthralled by the vast expanse of nature's finest to explore.

There is so much to see and do at just about every turn in this countryside, and there is plenty of history in the hills too, including some intriguing stories. We have incorporated places of history and interest into the walks.

Each of these walks has been specially surveyed for this book. Even where we were familiar with the routes, we have walked them again to ensure all the information is as up to date as possible. Unfortunately we cannot rule out the fact that changes to paths, gates and stiles are not infrequent.

These days many more people seem to be dog owners so a wider and more up market range of cafés and pubs are now allowing dogs inside their doors. Some of the previously more aloof establishments now realise that turning away dog owners means turning away a sizable trade. Also, dog-unfriendly stiles are being increasingly replaced with dog-friendly gates and more National Trust properties are allowing dogs into their grounds.

On the negative side, we have found a tendency for dog passages through or around stiles to be blocked and we have had to find alternative paths for you or discount the routes altogether. If you find your route obstructed by newly imposed obstructions, do not risk harming your animal by forcing them through or over them. If in any doubt about either the progress or safety of the route, or where a path has become unclear, obstructed or for some reason non-existent, always be prepared to turn round.

Before setting out always allow enough time to retrace your route before the onset of darkness. A sunny crisp winter's afternoon is a fantastic time of year to enjoy a dog walk, but don't forget how early it actually gets dark. Use common sense in relation to your safety and the safety of your dog.

The Surrey Hills – A Dog Walker's Guide

Before you set out always make sure you take the relevant Ordnance Survey map with you and you know how to read it – we always give details of the relevant sheet as part of the walk. The latest editions of the 1:25,000 series are by far the best.

In order to assist in satellite navigation to the start point of the walk, we have included the nearest postcode, although of course a postcode cannot always deliver you to a precise starting point, especially in rural areas.

David & Hilary Staines

ADVICE FOR DOG WALKERS

Obviously we want you and your dog to have an enjoyable and safe day out. The Countryside Code has published six steps to ensure your walk in the countryside is as safe as possible. These are:

1   Control your dog so that it does not scare or disturb farm animals or wildlife.
2   When using new access rights over open country and common land you must keep your dog on a short lead between 1 March and 31 July – and all year round near farm animals – and you may not be able to take your dog at all on some areas or at some times. Please follow any official signs.
3   You do not have to put your dog on a lead on public paths, as long as it is under close control. But, as a general rule, keep your dog on a lead if you cannot rely on its obedience. By law, farmers are entitled to destroy a dog that injures or worries their animals.
4   If a farm animal chases you and your dog, it is safer to let your dog off the lead – don't risk getting hurt by trying to protect it.
5   Take particular care that your dog doesn't scare sheep or lambs, or wander where it might disturb birds that nest on the ground and other wildlife – eggs and young will soon die without protection from their parents.
6   Everyone knows how unpleasant dog mess is and it can cause infections, so always clean up after your dog and get rid of the mess responsibly. Also make sure your dog is wormed regularly to protect it, other animals and people.

You can find out more about this advice from https://www.gov.uk/government/publications/the-countryside-code/the-countryside-code.

There is more advice from the Forestry Commission on what to do in an emergency on a day out. This book gives you contact details for the nearest vet on each walk but this information should help with an emergency before you can get advice from a vet.

Road Accidents, fractures and falls:
- Keep calm so as not to cause panic.
- Make sure you and your dog aren't in further danger; keep the dog warm.
- If you need to move the dog out of danger, do so slowly and gently. If it can't walk, use a coat, board or blanket as a stretcher.
- Try to stem blood flow from cuts with a pad and firm pressure: press

The Surrey Hills – A Dog Walker's Guide

around any foreign objects – such as broken glass or metal – to avoid pushing them further in.
- Dogs can appear paralysed after a severe accident, but this can be temporary. Never assume an animal is beyond help – follow veterinary advice.
- Internal injuries are not always obvious; contact your vet immediately if your pet is off colour within 24 hours of an accident.

Poisoning:
Many garden and agricultural chemicals can be attractive to dogs but fatal, so never let your dog out of sight or let it eat what it finds when out for a walk. If you think your dog has ingested something poisonous, phone the vet immediately and keep any labels, containers or samples with you to help the vet decide the best treatment. Do not make your dog sick without first consulting the vet.

Heat stroke:
This occurs when dogs are exercised in hot weather, or left in cars on even moderately warm days. They will pant excessively and may vomit, collapse, have fits or difficulty breathing. If heat stroke occurs:

1 Keep the dog calm. Move it into the shade, a cool building or room, or near a fan or breeze.
2 Cool all of your dog with water, paying particular attention to the head.
3 Let your dog drink small amounts of cool water frequently. Call a vet.

Well, that's the serious bit out of the way. Now enjoy a guided doggie roam around some of the best places in England for walking your dog.

Abinger Hammer & Friday Street

Taking a dip in the River Tillingbourne.

This walk takes you to some of **Surrey Hills'** classic villages and hamlets. You can enjoy fine views of the Downs and visit the hamlet of Abinger Common with its village church and stocks. An extension of the walk will take you to one of the lesser-known but equally picturesque locations in the hills – Friday Street. This isolated hamlet with its handful of cottages is nestled in its own quiet secluded valley overlooking a mill pond.

The Surrey Hills – A Dog Walker's Guide

Terrain
A complete variety of terrains will be encountered on this walk. There is a little road walking (more so on the extension to Friday Street), but the main walk concentrates on paths and tracks through open fields and through woodland. You will climb a few gentle hills, but you will also be walking along the valley bottom through which the River Tillingbourne flows.

Where to park
There is a free village car park in Abinger Hammer on the main A25 road (GR TQ 096474).

How to get there
Sat Nav RH5 6RX. Abinger Hammer is on the main A25 Dorking to Guildford Road. The car park is in the centre of the village. Follow the signpost for Holmbury St Mary and the car park is a few yards down the road on the left just across the stream. **OS maps:** This walk crosses the divide between Exploreres 145 Guildford & Farnham and 146 Dorking, Box Hill & Reigate.

Nearest refreshments
The Abinger Hatch pub (☎ 01306 730737, theabingerhatch.com) is at point 3 on the walk. There is a great garden outside facing directly onto the church and village stocks. For a real hidden gem, try the Stephan Langton Inn (☎ 01306 730775, stephanlangton.pub) at Friday Street which bills itself as "the most secluded pub and restaurant in Surrey". Dogs are allowed in the bar area. For opening times and menus, see the website.

Dog factors
Distance: 4.5 miles / 7.2 km, or 5.5 miles / 8.9 km for the extended version.
Road walking: Short distances at a few points and one busy road to cross twice.
Livestock: None encountered, but there is a potential for seasonal grazing at a few locations.
Stiles: Only one that would be an issue for a larger dog (note the short diversion to avoid it in the text).
Nearest vets: Brelades, Station Road, Gomshall, Surrey, GU5 9LE.
☎ 01483 205066.

Abinger Hammer & Friday Street

The Walk

1 From the village car park and with the village green facing you, turn left up **Felday Road**. Take the next footpath on the left, crossing the stile. When the footpath emerges onto a field, the path can be indistinct, so you need to cross the field bearing to your right. When you have walked uphill a little you will see a footpath signpost to the right of the telegraph pole. Cross the stile. Keep going in the same direction, keeping to the right of the fence line. Half way up the hill the path switches from the right-hand side to the left-hand side of the fence. Keep going in the same direction when a bridleway joins from the left. Where another path joins on the right, keep ahead and cross the next field.

2 At the lane, turn right and then immediately left. Once in the farmyard turn right following the signs. When you have passed the buildings, the path turns sharp left. You now follow this path all the way to **Abinger Common**. Walk

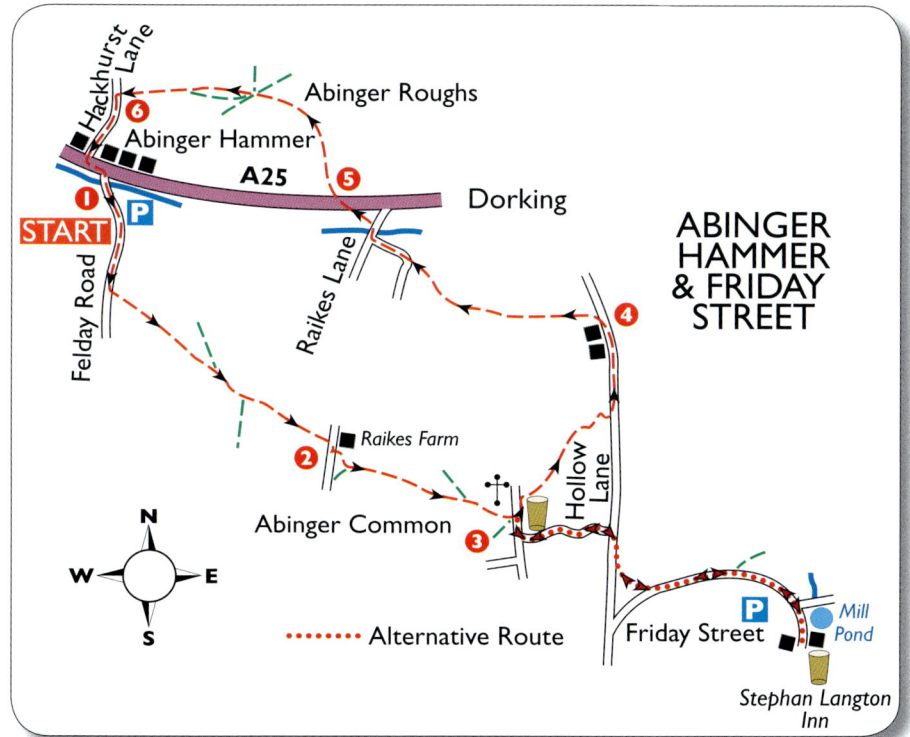

The Surrey Hills – A Dog Walker's Guide

Walking beside the mill pond at Friday Street.

past the church and you will be in the centre of the tiny village. *The church is a Grade II listed building with an 11th-century nave. The chancel and north chapel were built around 1220. It was bombed in the Second World War and restored in the 1950s. On the left-hand side of the green in front of the church you can see the village stocks. Thought to date from the 1770s they are very unusual as they can accommodate three people being pilloried at a time and include a whipping post.*

❸ With the **Abinger Hatch** pub facing you, turn left, walk down the lane a few yards and take the slip road on the right. Turn immediately right and then bear left along the footpath. Continue along this path. Bear right where another path diverges left and follow the path all the way down through the woods to the road. At the road (**Hollow Lane**), turn left.

If you wish to extend the walk to **Friday Street**, turn right opposite the pub in **Abinger Common** (point 3) and take the next road on the left. At the end of this road, turn right and then take the footpath up through the woods

Abinger Hammer & Friday Street

on the left. When this emerges onto a lane turn left. After a while there will be a parallel path on the right-hand side of the road. Follow the road down to the bottom and you will be facing the picturesque mill pond – another remnant of the iron industry. The narrow road on the right which rises gently past the cottages is the way to the **Stephan Langton** pub which is just a few yards further on.

4 At the end of the row of cottages take the path on the left. Follow this track through the woods until it emerges onto a road. Cross the stile and keep going along the road in the same direction. At the end of the road turn right into **Raikes Lane**. As soon as you have crossed the river, take the footpath on the left. The stile here may be problematic for larger dogs. (If you can't get through just walk the few yards down to the main road and turn left to regain the route.) Cross the field. At the other side, cross the main road and then take the footpath opposite. Take care as this is a busy road with fast moving traffic.

5 You now follow this path as it twists behind some back gardens, through some trees and out into an open valley. The path enters an area where the trees are marked by a National Trust sign marking Abinger Roughs. Keep going in the same direction when you cross the clearing at **Broomy Downs**. The path enters the woods straight ahead of you. Keep going ahead and at the other side of the wood views of the nearby Downs will open up on your right. The path drops gently down the open hillside. Go through the gate at the bottom keeping in the same direction.

6 When you emerge onto **Hackhurst Lane**, turn left and follow it to the bottom. At the end turn left and you will see the car park across the green ahead of you. *You can't fail to notice the marvellous clock on the corner of the building which overhangs the main road. The figure is Jack the Blacksmith, who strikes the hour with his hammer. The clock bears the inscription "By me you know how fast to go". It was given in memory of the first Lord Farrer of Abinger Hall who died in 1899 and it represents the once thriving local iron industry.*

Alfold

One of the canal mileposts deep inside Sidney Wood.

This is a delightful and relaxing walk, mostly through woodland, but also along what remains of the winding course of the Wey and Arun Canal. You will discover not only these remains, but also encounter the renovations under way, which aim to rebuild this historic canal for use in the 21st century.

Terrain
Flat and easy walking along mostly wooded canal paths or quiet byways.

Where to park
Park at the Sidney Wood car park (GR TQ 026352).

Alfold ②

How to get there
Sat Nav GU6 8JG. From Guildford take the A281 south to Alfold Crossways. Here turn right following the sign for Loxwood, but immediately sharp right again along Dunsfold Road. Follow the road as it turns sharp left a few hundred yards later. The car park is on the left-hand side where the road bears right. **OS map:** OL34 Crawley & Horsham.

Nearest refreshments
The Sir Roger Tichborne (☎ 01403 751873, www.thetichborne.co.uk) pub is in the village of Alfold Bars. You can take a very short diversion off the walk to get there. Established in 1873, and recently refurbished, it prides itself as being an independent, family-run countryside pub.

Dog factors

Distance: 6 miles / 9.7 km.
Road walking: A couple of short stretches.
Livestock: Take great care of horses in the proximity of Turtles Farm which is a working equestrian centre where horses will be grazing or being trained in the adjacent fields. It is wise to keep your dog on a lead here.
Stiles: None.
Nearest vets: Alfold Veterinary Surgery, Unit 13, Alfold Business Centre, Loxwood Road, Alfold, GU6 8HP. ☎ 01403 753 500.

The Walk

❶ Walk out of the car park and bear left. A few yards later dog-leg sharp left down the drive signposted **Sedgehurst Private**. The blue waymarker confirms that this is a footpath right of way. A few hundred yards later, turn right off the footpath following the **Wey-South** waymarker. Follow the path through the woods passing **Fir Tree Copse** and the **Surrey Wildlife Trust information board** on your right. Continue along the path and at the next divergence bear right following the light blue waymarker. Continue through the wood passing through the metal gate where you have the course of the old canal on your right-hand side. *The 23-mile Wey & Arun Canal was once the country's only canal connection to the English Channel. Now known as London's lost route to the sea it opened in 1816. Its success was short-lived. Once the railways became established, it was unable to compete and was abandoned in 1871. The canal lay derelict for*

15

The Surrey Hills – A Dog Walker's Guide

nearly 100 years until 1970 when the Wey and Arun Canal Trust was established with the aim of restoring it.

❷ Crossing over the course of the old canal, turn sharp left onto the old canal towpath with the course of the canal now on your left. Follow the course of the canal as it twists and turns through **Sidney Wood**. Continue through the woods keeping the course of the canal on your left-hand side until you

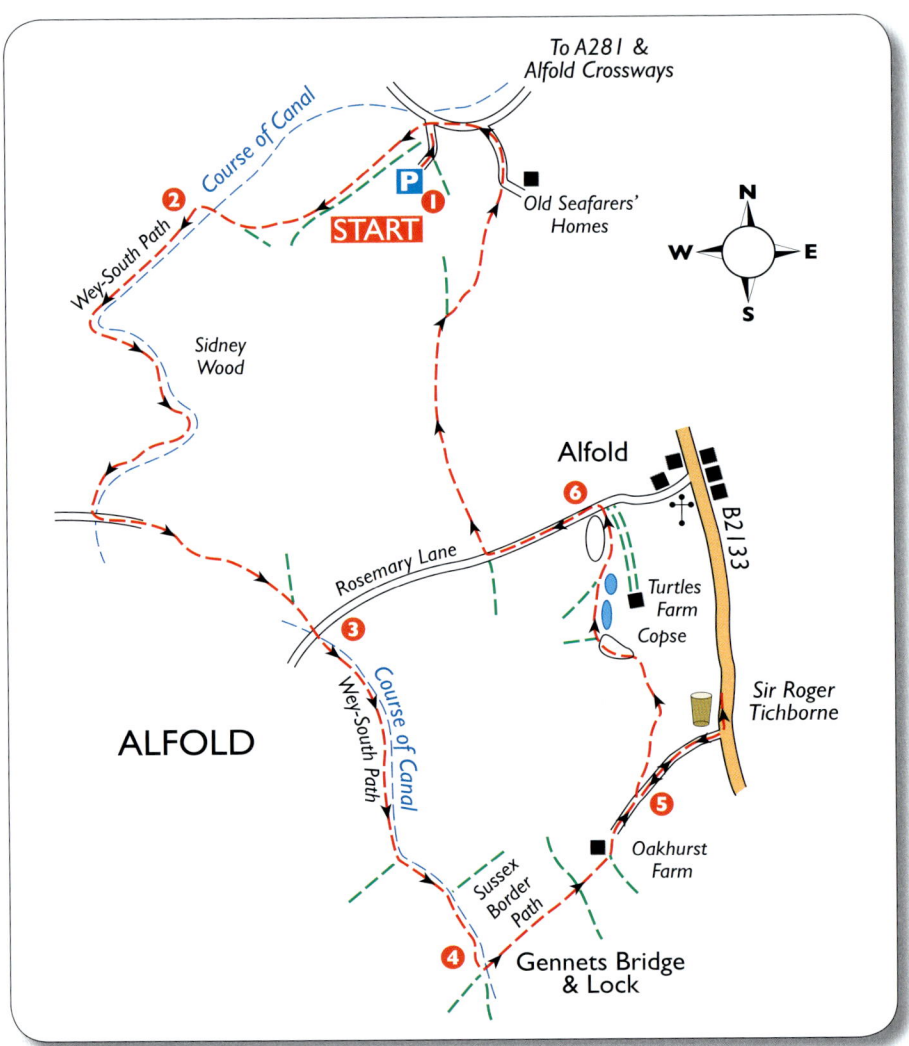

Alfold 2

emerge onto a tarmac track. Turn left here again, following the Wey-South waymarker. Continue along the track as it passes through the woods. When it finally emerges at a gate, continue ahead with the large White House on your right.

3 With the house on your right, when you come to the road, turn right and then sharp left following the footpath sign. You will now have the course of the canal again on your left-hand side. Keep ahead until you reach the crossroads with the Sussex Border Path at **Gennets Bridge and Lock**. *The new bridge and lock here were completed in 2018 and it's a refreshing contrast to the derelict course of the canal that you have been walking along.*

4 Turn left over the new bridge now following the **Sussex Border Path**. At the crossroads of paths with the farm in the distance, keep ahead. Skirt **Oakhurst Farm** on the left-hand side and drop down towards the gate. Go through the gate and bear right along the lane. If you wish to visit the **Sir Roger**

Near point 3 the canal on the right is just a dry imprint at Gennets Wood.

The Surrey Hills – A Dog Walker's Guide

Titchborne pub, just keep going straight ahead up the lane. At the end of the lane, turn left on the main road and the pub is a few yards ahead on the left-hand side.

5 A few yards later, turn left following the footpath sign. Go through the gate and keep ahead along the wide grassy track. Go through the next gate, keeping the field line on the right-hand side. At the next gate, bear slightly left following the black footpath waymarker crossing diagonally over the field. At the end, go through the gate into the copse, but then bear immediately left. Follow the path through the copse bearing left over the tiny wooden bridge over a small stream. Now keep ahead with the fence line on your left. When you emerge from the copse at the stile, turn sharp right. The path is now indistinct, but you need to keep to the right-hand field boundary. You will have the ponds of **Turtles Farm** on your right-hand side. You should keep your dog on a lead as horses may be grazing here. At the next small gate, keep going ahead. You will soon have the field boundary on your right and a horse exercise track on your left. Keep going to the very end and at the gate turn left.

6 Continue down **Rosemary Lane** for a few hundred yards. There is a wide wooded verge on the left-hand side. Take the next footpath on the right and follow this through the woods right to the very end. The entrance to the old seafarers' homes will diverge from the right. Keep ahead along the lane and when you come to the road turn left. A short distance later, turn left into the car park to return to the start.

Banstead Woods

The woods are famed for carpets of bluebells in springtime.

Banstead Woods has a long history going back to Norman times. Over the years, it has been in the ownership of kings and queens, and knights of the realm. It is famous for the carpets of bluebells in spring, and now it has a unique set of *The Lion, the Witch and the Wardrobe*-themed chainsaw sculptures. This is a fairly short walk with a pub to visit on the way – ideal for a Sunday, either to work up an appetite or to work off a lunch!

Terrain
Footpaths and tracks through the woods and later along the wide grassy slopes of Chipstead Valley. A couple of short, sharp gradients.

The Surrey Hills – A Dog Walker's Guide

Where to park
There is a large free car park on Holly Lane (GR TQ 27295 58329).

How to get there
Sat Nav CR5 3NR. From the M25 junction 8 take the A217 northbound. At the first roundabout turn round and double back the way you have come. Just before you return to the M25, turn left along Blackhorse Lane. Now follow this road right into Chipstead Village. Just before the White Hart pub, turn left into Hazelwood Lane. Follow this to the very end and at the roundabout on the B2032 turn right. Take the next left into Lower Park Road (B2219) and the car park is on the left-hand side. **OS map:** Explorer 146 Dorking, Box Hill & Reigate.

Nearest refreshments
The Rambler's Rest (☎ 01737 552661, www.theramblersrest.co.uk) is at point 5 on the walk. It describes itself as "Bringing together elements of rustic charm and modern flair". The pub features an attractive outside terrace. Please check the website for opening times and the menu.

Dog factors
Distance: 2.5 miles / 4 km.
Road walking: None.
Livestock: None encountered.
Stiles: None.
Nearest vets: Anwell Veterinary Centre, 41 Brighton Road, Coulsdon, Surrey, CR5 2BF. ☎ 020 86686151.

The Walk

1 Take the path leading uphill away from the car park, which passes the picnic area on the left. Passing the carved lamp post, take the fork of the path up into the woods. The characters from *The Lion, the Witch and the Wardrobe* feature in a Narnia-themed nature trail. *Sculptures include Lucy Pevensie waiting by the lamp post, while Aslan the lion guards the entrance to the wood. Later on, you can walk through the wardrobe entrance to Narnia, complete with wooden hanging coats. See if you can spot the witch in the wood. The figures have been carved out of existing standing dead trees by a highly skilled chainsaw sculptor. Carved posts depicting the area's special flora and fauna can also be found in the woods.* At the lion sculpture, keep ahead walking up the hill. Where the gradient evens out, turn right at the next main path at marker post **No 2**. There is a bench at the

Banstead Woods ③

junction of paths. Continue along this path with the witch sculpture set back in the woods on your right and the wardrobe on your left. Continue ahead past marker **No 3**.

② Where the path drops slightly downhill and there is a fork, turn right and a few paces later, at marker **No 4**, turn sharp left. Carry on steadily up the gentle hill, following the path as it narrows until the far end where a path comes in from the right. Here bear left. Continue over the crossroads of paths, pass marker **No 12** and keep ahead. *Banstead Woods' recorded history stretches back for nearly a thousand years, to the time of the Domesday Book (AD 1086). Both King Edward I and II gave the woods to their wives, and hunted here for deer. Catherine of Aragon, Henry VIII's first wife, was the last Queen to have the woods as a gift. She owned the woods until her death in 1536. Saved from housing development, in 1934 the woods were bought by Surrey County Council for everyone to enjoy.*

③ A few yards after you pass a fenced pond on the left there is a fork. Take the right-hand narrower path. A few paces later at the next fork, turn left. Continue along this path through the woods until the paths diverge. Here, take the broader path out into the open. Follow this through an area of scrub until it emerges out onto the hillside. Keep in the same direction, continuing down the hill and go through the gate ahead.

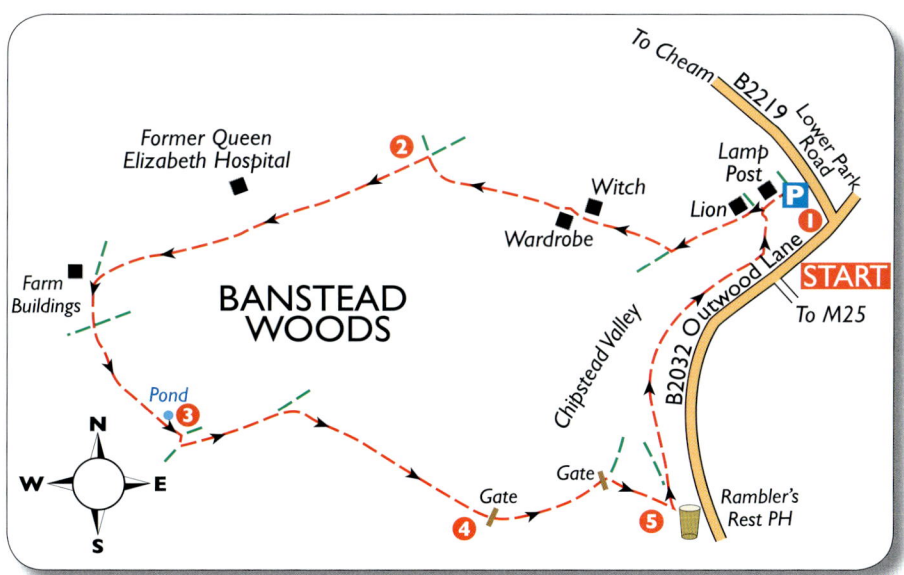

The Surrey Hills – A Dog Walker's Guide

④ Continue through the gate following the path as it swings left. At the next gate, turn right down the hill. The **Rambler's Rest pub** is at the bottom of the hill.

⑤ To continue the walk, once you are at the gate at the back of the pub, turn left and take the lower of the two paths across the grassy field. Continue ahead keeping the road to your right. Follow this path parallel to the road until you come to a fork with a broad grassy path turning steeply uphill. Follow this and once the gradient levels out, you will see the car park on your right.

Lucy Pevensie waiting by the lamp post on the Narnia-themed nature trail.

Box Hill

Crossing the stepping stones.

This walk takes you along some of the most popular paths in the Surrey Hills. The hill takes its name from the ancient box woodland found on its steepest slopes where some of the trees are over 1,000 years old. The western part of the hill is one of the most popular locations in the area with an estimated 850,000 visitors per year. This means that it can get very crowded at peak times. Don't bother coming here on sunny Sunday afternoons in summer – the place will be heaving and the car parks will be

The Surrey Hills – A Dog Walker's Guide

full. On these days, just choose another walk. That is not to detract from the enjoyment of the walk at quieter times. There is plenty to see and it takes in some of the famous sights of the Hills.

Dog factors

Distance: 4.5 miles / 7.2 km.
Road walking: About a quarter of a mile along a very quiet road. Plus, a few yards at one point on the pavement next to the busy A24.
Livestock: None encountered.
Stiles: None.
Nearest vets: Brelades, 20 Knoll Road, Dorking, Surrey RH4 3EP. ☎ 01306 883086.

Terrain

There is real variety here. The route takes you from the top of the Downs to the very bottom, encompassing hillside and riverside walks. There is a steep route down and very steep uphill return. There is a small amount of road walking but most of the route is along waymarked paths.

Where to park

The main car park is opposite the visitors' centre. Charges apply for non-National Trust members (GR: TQ 178513).

How to get there

Sat Nav KT20 7LB. Follow the signs for Box Hill on the main A24 road; one mile north of Dorking, 2.5 miles south of Leatherhead. Turn right onto the famous Zig Zag Road, and follow the road for 1.5 miles to the top. Although on a much smaller scale, this road has been likened to roads in the French Alps. Once you have reached the information centre, parking is on the left-hand side. **OS map:** Explorer 146 Dorking, Box Hill & Reigate.

Nearest refreshments

There is a National Trust café at the visitors' centre, with benches and tables outside where you can sit with your dog. There is a separate outside servery as well. To avoid the crowds, order your food to take away and carry it to the viewpoint at point 2. Here, there is plenty of space to sit on the grassy side of the hill.

Box Hill 4

The Walk

1 From the car park cross the road and facing the café, turn left. Follow the path running parallel to the trees. It will quickly emerge at **Salomons Memorial** viewpoint. Just below the memorial, take the path on the right. At the next junction of paths take the left-hand turn with the pink National Trust waymarker.

2 Follow this path as it drops down the hill. At the far end of the path turn right into **Boxhill Road**. Continue down the road under the railway bridge and, where the road bears left, continue ahead until you reach the river.

3 Turn right onto the riverside path. You will now keep to this path with the **River Mole** on your left. You will pass **Pixham Weir**. *The mill on the opposite bank dates from 1837 and was in use until 1937. The river turned several waterwheels principally for grinding corn and cleaning cloth.* After you have walked underneath the railway at **Pixham Viaduct**, look up to the top of the hillside on the right. *The ornate Swiss Cottage was the home of John Logie Baird, the inventor of the first working television system, between 1929 and 1932. He conducted some of his experiments on Box Hill.* After a while the path leaves the riverside and climbs up into the woods.

4 At the end it emerges onto a stepped path. Turn left down the steps, now ignoring the pink waymarker. Once the path has flattened out there is a fork signed left for the stepping stones or right for the footbridge. Keep left and the stones will shortly be ahead of you. If you want to cross the stones with your dog, continue across the water. It can get busy here – if your dog falls in, or you do, you will probably do so in front of an audience! *A ford here across the River Mole is thought to have existed since prehistoric times although the stones were first recorded in 1841. The current stepping stones were added in 1946, replacing those removed during the Second World War as an anti-invasion measure.* If you don't fancy the crossing (or at times when the water level is high and flowing over the top of them), take the fork in the path you passed earlier and cross the river by the bridge. Once past the bridge, carry on along the broad path across the field with the river on your right. The path brings you up to the busy A24 road.

5 Bear immediately right on the A24 along the pavement, crossing the river and passing in front of the Burford Bridge Hotel. Immediately after you have passed the hotel, take the footpath on the right which heads very steeply uphill. Where the paths immediately diverge, bear left and head straight up the hillside. The gradient here is very steep. There is a slightly easier

The Surrey Hills – A Dog Walker's Guide

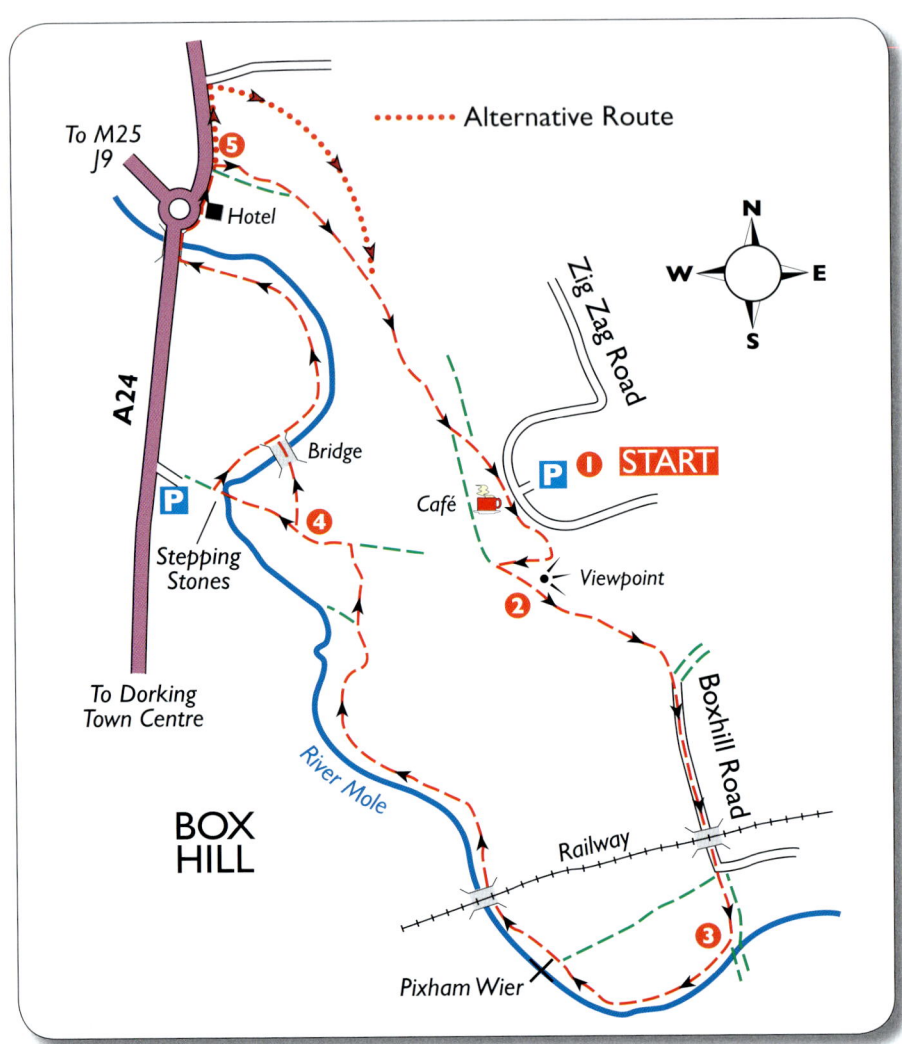

path further along the road on the right. As you emerge onto the broad grassy area and the gradient levels out, keep the bush line on your right-hand side. You will see purple National Trust waymarkers; follow these up the hill, eventually taking a path through a gate. Shortly after the gate, take the left-hand (slightly lower) fork in the path, which will take you past the remains of Box Hill Fort. *It was one of 13 London Defence Positions built to protect the capital from invasion from Europe. Construction began in 1896 yet after only*

Box Hill

10 years a change in defence policy saw the scheme abandoned and most of the forts were sold back to the original landowners. Box Hill fort was an infantry redoubt, and included magazines for the storage of artillery ammunition. The fort had no large guns on site, it was designed to be a base for mobile field artillery which would be deployed nearby as required. A network of trenches linking the forts would be quickly dug if an invasion threat became imminent. Internally the building has been abandoned as it is inhabited by several species of protected bats. A few yards further up the hill will bring you back to the start.

The view from Box Hill overlooking the town of Dorking.

Chinthurst Hill

The Victorian folly at the top of the hill.

This is by far the shortest walk in the book, fairly centrally placed in the Hills and ideal when you just want a quick trip out. Although short it contains all the ingredients of a traditional Surrey Hills walk. It loops up and around Chinthurst Hill, with some marvellous views, some glimpses of an historic Lutyens country house and the chance to view a Victorian folly tower at the summit of the hill.

Terrain
With well-maintained paths, this route encompasses a trail maintained by the Surrey Wildlife Trust. There is a steep gradient with some steps.

Chinthurst Hill 5

Dog factors

Distance: 1.5 miles / 2.4 km.
Road walking: None.
Livestock: The Surrey Wildlife Trust warns that animals sometimes graze at the top of Chinthurst Hill.
Stiles: None.
Nearest vets: Oak Barn Vets, Tilehouse Barn, East Shalford Lane, Guildford GU4 8AE. ☎ 01483 455355.

Where to park
There is a free car park at Chinthurst Hill, off the Kings Road/B2128, a couple of miles south of Guildford (GR TQ 014462).

How to get there
Sat Nav GU5 0PR. From the south take the A281. At Bramley take the right turn for Wonersh. Once in Wonersh village follow Wonersh Common Road/B2128 and it is on the left-hand side of the road. From Guildford and the north, take the A281 and then take the A248. Continue ahead along the B2128 and it is immediately on the right. **OS map:** Explorer 145 Guildford & Farnham.

Nearest refreshments
The attractive looking timbered Grantley Arms (☎ 01483 893351, thegrantleyarms.co.uk) in Wonersh has been part of village life for half a millennium. Dogs are welcome in the large open bar and there is pleasant outside terrace seating as well. For menu details and the opening times, check the website. Directions from the walk: turn right out of the car park, keep going and the pub will be facing you when you get to the village centre. The pub has its own small car park.

The Walk

1 Leave the car park at the opposite end to the entrance and walk up into the trees. After a few yards you will come to a junction of paths, here you need to turn left. Continue up into the wood and at the divergence of paths bear right.

2 A few paces later, at the crossroads of paths, turn right following the green

The Surrey Hills – A Dog Walker's Guide

waymarker. Follow this path as it meanders through the woods until it emerges into a clearing with a tarmac drive in front of you.

❸ Turn sharp left here and immediately left again through the gate and past the noticeboard. Again, carry on following this track, then take the next footpath on the right-hand side signposted 'to tower'. Climb up through the woods until you reach the clearing with Chinthurst Hill Tower on your right-hand side. *Many believe that the tower was built in the 1930s by Lord Inchcape, the then owner of Chinthurst Hill house, but Historic England have the Grade II listed sandstone folly as being of late 19th-century origin.* In front of the tower there is an orientation stone showing the direction and distance to many landmarks of the Surrey Hills. To your right, you can glimpse **Chinthurst Hill** through the trees. *Chinthurst Hill house was the first major commission of the iconic architect Sir Edwin Lutyens and has been described as being situated on 'the finest*

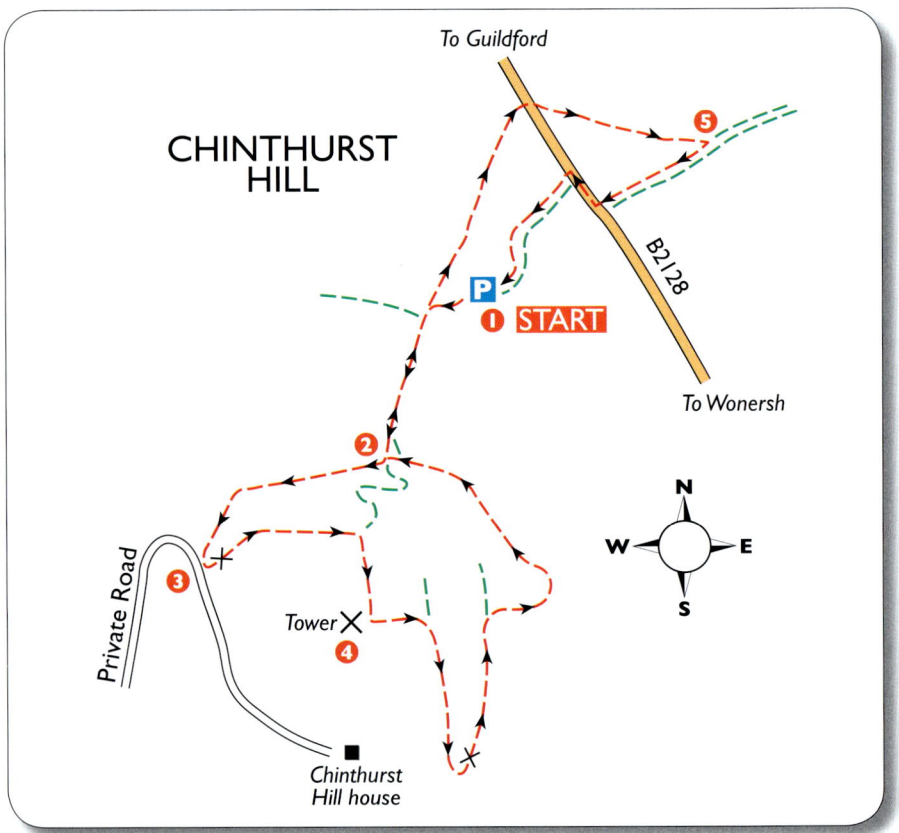

Chinthurst Hill 5

site in the South of England'. It was built in 1893-1895 and the bargate stone for the building was quarried from the hillside.

4 With your back to the tower, walk past the orientation stone again following the green waymarker towards the woods. Do not enter the woods, but instead turn right down the broad green track and follow this as it drops gently downhill. Continue as it loops around to the left and go through the gate and carry on with the field line on your right-hand side. On your right, enjoy more views of the Hills. Where the field line turns sharp right, follow the path again as it starts to drop down the hillside, in places quite steeply. You now follow the path back to point 2. Now turn right down the path you originally walked up, but instead of turning right back into the car park, keep ahead along this track until you emerge onto **Kings Road**. Cross the road and go into the woods of **Wonersh Common**.

5 When you emerge onto a tarmac drive, turn right. Continue to the end of the road then turn right and next left back along the road into the car park.

Devil's Punch Bowl

Looking across the Devil's Punchbowl at the beginning of the walk.

The Devil's Punch Bowl is one of the most popular spots in the Surrey Hills. It is either the floor of what was once a giant cavern that collapsed after water springs had hollowed it out, or alternatively it is the imprint of the Devil's backside when he landed here, having jumped from the Devil's Dyke on the south coast. Whichever account you believe, this is a walk that takes you to one of the most famous locations in the Surrey Hills.

Terrain
This is essentially a woodland walk which also uses paths and tracks, with some steep gradients in places.

Where to park
Park in the National Trust car park just off the old A3. Free for National Trust members, non-members have to pay (GR SU 890357).

Devil's Punch Bowl 6

How to get there
Sat Nav GU26 6AG. From the A3 take the junction south of Hindhead tunnel, following the signs for Hindhead. Once you have left the main road, follow the brown tourist signs for the Devil's Punch Bowl. Once you are in the village, cross over both mini roundabouts and the car park is on the left-hand side. **OS map:** Explorer OL33 Haslemere & Petersfield.

Nearest refreshments
There is a new National Trust café at the car park. There are plenty of benches under the trees where you can sit with your dog.

Dog factors
Distance: 2.5 miles / 4 km.
Road walking: Along the old turnpike road (which is closed to normal traffic) and along a very quiet lane.
Livestock: The potential for horses towards the end of the walk on Hindhead Common.
Stiles: None.
Nearest vets: Amery Veterinary Group, Ashburnham House, Crossways Road, Grayshott, Hampshire, GU26 6HJ.
☎ 01428 604442.

The Walk

1 With the café facing you turn right and head towards the open space and the viewing platform. Give yourself a few minutes here to take in the views. At the viewpoint, turn around and now facing the café retrace your steps a few yards to the large signpost. Much, but not all of this walk will follow the trail shown by a black arrow on a pink waymarker. After a short while you will cross the course of the old A3 main road. Keep ahead along the path and a short distance later turn left along the broad concrete path – this is the old turnpike road. *This marks the spot where the first road built to connect London and Portsmouth passed over the hills of Hindhead. This part of the road was a favourite haunt of highwaymen. By the early 1700s increasing traffic had caused roads to deteriorate so much that turnpike trusts were set up to maintain them and charge tolls. The road here underwent this process in 1749. However, by the 1820s, it could no longer cope with the levels of traffic and was re-routed to a lower path around the rim of the Punch Bowl. History repeated itself when in 2011 this new road had also*

The Surrey Hills – A Dog Walker's Guide

become choked with traffic and it was replaced by a tunnel underneath the hill.

2 Keep ahead, after a while passing the **Sailor's Stone** on your left-hand side. *The stone commemorates the events of 24th September 1786 when an unknown sailor walking to Portsmouth befriended three men in a local pub. He bought them food and drink. When he left and was walking along the turnpike road, they followed him, robbing him of his money and clothes before cutting his throat. Take a look at the curse inscribed on the back of the stone. A short distance further, there is an original mile post from the turnpike road. To your left you will have views through the trees of the* **Punch Bowl**.

3 After a short while, turn sharp right following the pink and black arrow waymarker. The path takes a short, but steep gradient up the steps and comes out at the Celtic Cross and viewpoint. *Criminals were hanged and their tarred bodies left in a gibbet, an open metal cage, to swing in chains until they rotted. It was designed as a warning to highwaymen and others with criminal intent. Here the bodies of the three men convicted of the sailor's murder were hung in gibbets for three years until they were brought down by a storm. Although today this is a place to stop and enjoy the magnificent views, in the 19th century it had a*

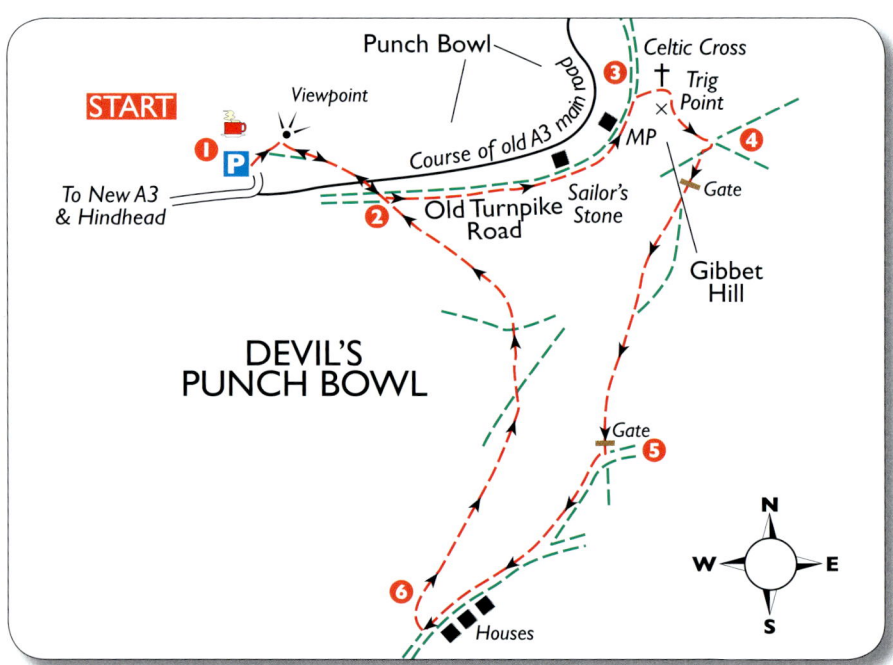

Devil's Punch Bowl

reputation for being haunted. In 1851, the granite Celtic cross was erected as an attempt to dispel the fear of local people. With the trigonometry point to the right, follow the pink and black arrow waymarker into the woods. The path drops steeply down. At the bottom of the valley you come to a junction of five paths and you stop following the pink waymarker.

4 At the junction, turn right and then bear immediately left, following the blue waymarker. Drop down the hill through the gate. Where the paths diverge again (now confusingly with blue waymarkers in both directions) keep right. Follow this path right to the point where there is a gate which comes out onto a lane.

5 Go through the gate and you are now back with the pink and black arrow waymarkers. Follow the pink and black waymarkers, turning right up the hill. Continue some distance up the hill.

6 At the top, follow the pink and black waymarker through the gate on the right-hand side. Continue following the pink and black trail which will eventually bring you out on a section of **Hindhead Common**. We found horses grazing here. Go through the gate and you will be back on the old turnpike road at point 2. Now retrace your steps back to the start.

The course of the old trunk A3 road, this now green and secluded spot was once choked with traffic which now passes through tunnels beneath the hill.

Farnham

The imposing castle ruins overlooking the west end of the park.

This is a walk in the park – but no ordinary park. Farnham Park is both a historic deer park and a local nature reserve covering an enormous 320 acres. It's a mixture of rolling fields, grassland, ancient trees, streams and ponds. The walk takes you through a variety of these landscapes including an impressive tree-lined avenue that goes on for half a mile. Although it is possible to just walk on tarmac paths around the park's perimeter, we have chosen a slightly shorter route that gives you more variety, using paths through some of the woods and grasslands.

Farnham 7

Terrain
Mostly level footpaths, although there is a stretch that undulates slightly. There are livestock grazing areas in the park, but this walk keeps you away from them.

Where to park
There is a free car park at the Park Office & Information Centre, on the opposite side of the drive to the cricket ground (GR SU 837475).

How to get there
Sat Nav GU9 0AU. From the A31, take the A325 into Farnham town centre. Turn into Castle Street and keep going up Castle Hill. Once you have passed the castle, the car park is on the right. **OS Map:** Explorer 145 Guildford & Farnham.

Nearest refreshments
The Park Café is just a few yards from the starting point of the walk, just follow the signpost. The building is not obvious to find, as its entrance and terrace face away from the park. You know it's going to be dog friendly when you see a water bowl at every outside table. For more information, visit www.fpgc.co.uk/park-cafe.

Dog factors
Distance: 2 miles / 4 km.
Road walking: None.
Livestock: None.
Stiles: None.
Nearest vets: Castle Vets in Farnham, 131 Upper Hale Road, Farnham, GU9 0JG. ☎ 01252 718128.

The Walk

1 At the end of the car park, turn right following the **Farnham Castle** signpost. Keep the cricket ground on your right and head towards the castle. *The magnificent medieval motte and bailey castle has stood over the park since the 12th century. It was founded in 1138 by Henry of Blois, Bishop of Winchester and brother of King Stephen. In medieval times the diocese of Winchester was the richest in England, and Farnham was a favourite residence of the bishops. Next door is the Bishops' Palace, a mix of Norman, Tudor and Restoration building*

The Surrey Hills – A Dog Walker's Guide

styles. The Castle's history and location so close to the deer park has made the park one of the most important historic landscapes in the south of England.

❷ Turn down the long avenue of trees and continue until the very end. The avenue was planted on the orders of Bishop Morley in the 17th century, although the original elms have been replaced with lime and beech trees.

❸ At the end, turn left along a tarmac path and, a few yards later, when the path heads into the trees, take the path that turns left. Keep on the path to

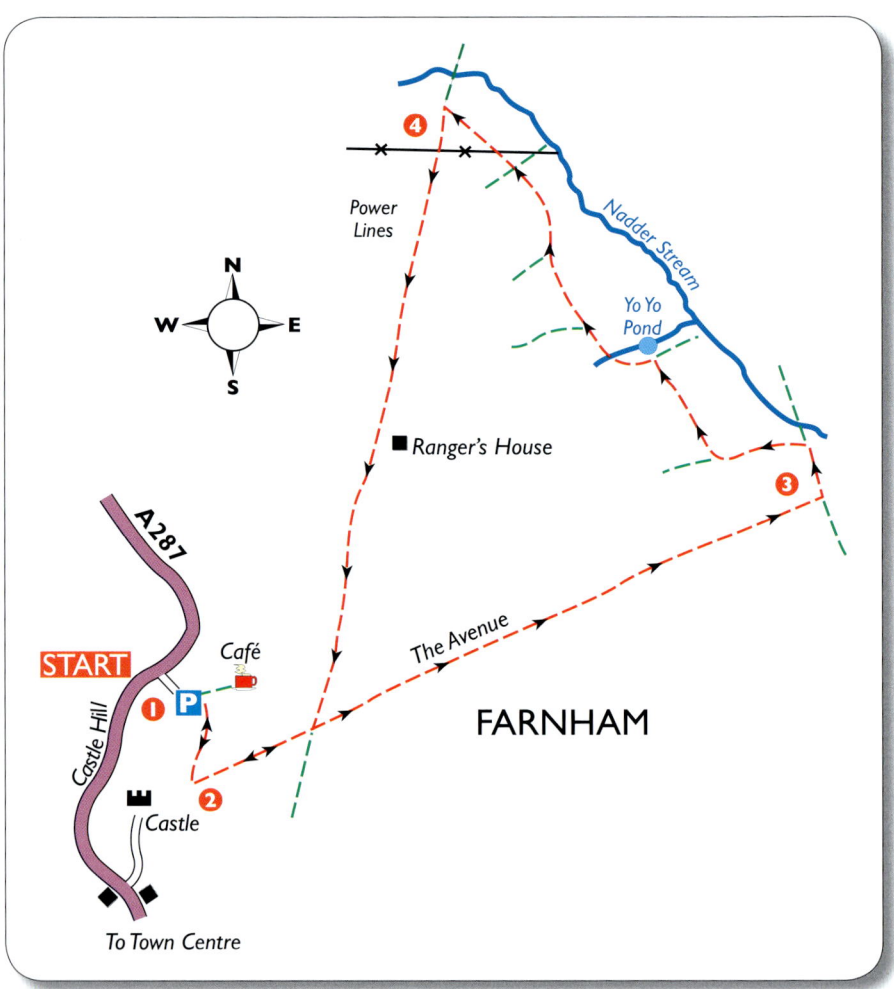

Farnham

the right of the gate. Continue along this path as it meanders through the woods, always keeping the cattle fence to your immediate left. The path will eventually bring you away from the fence and up into a field. Ignore the fainter path to the left and keep to the right-hand side of the field boundary and follow it as it turns and until you find yourself underneath the power lines.

4 Shortly after you have passed beneath the power lines, turn left onto the tarmac path and you will pass back underneath the wires. Continue back along this path which will eventually bring you back to the tree avenue. Then, turn right and retrace your steps. *Farnham Park was "emparked" by Bishop Wykeham in 1376, with a wooden 'pale' or fence keeping the deer in and the locals out. The Ranger's House, which you passed on your left, was built in the 17th century to keep poachers and squatters out. For over 600 years, Farnham Park was a private domain visited by royalty and the nobility. During the First World War horses were grazed here to get them fit before being sent to France.*

Newlands Corner & St Martha's Hill

The view from Newlands Corner looking towards Albury.

This is a classic Surrey Hills walk through woods and open fields where you can enjoy outstanding views over the Downs. The walk starts from Newlands Corner for one of the most iconic views over the Surrey hills. You also have the opportunity to visit the ancient church of Saint Martha. Perched high upon its hill, it was a resting point for travellers on the Pilgrims' Way.

Newlands Corner & St Martha's Hill (8)

Terrain
This is an undulating walk, as you would expect of the Surrey Hills, with a few moderately steep, but steady gradients. Apart from one very short stretch of less than 100 yards along a quiet lane, the walk is entirely off road using footpaths and broad tracks. Because of the local sandstone, you will be walking on sand in places.

Where to park
There is a large car park at Newlands Corner, off the A25. At the time of writing, parking was free, but Surrey County Council had announced plans to charge for parking with a four-hour maximum stay (GR TQ 042492).

How to get there
Sat Nav GU4 8SE. Newlands Corner is on the A25. From the A3, take the B2215 to the village of Send Marsh. Then follow the A247 through Clandon, which will become the A25 after it crosses the A246. After the crossing, Newlands Corner is just over a mile further on, with the main car park on the right. **OS Map:** Explorer 145 Guildford and Farnham.

Nearest refreshments
There is a café next to the visitor centre with outside tables. On the other side of the A25 road is the Squirrel Hill Café where dogs are welcome at the outside tables. For more information, visit www.squirrel-hill.co.uk.

Dog factors
Distance: 4 miles / 6.4 km.
Road walking: A short distance of less than 100 yards.
Livestock: None, but some of the walk is along bridle paths, so expect the occasional horse and rider.
Stiles: None.
Nearest vets: The Cape Veterinary Clinic, 174 Epsom Rd, Guildford, GU1 2RR. ☎ 01483 538990.

The Walk

1 Walk back towards the main road and, at the entrance to the car park, turn right, following the green waymarker. *Newlands Corner is renowned for superb views across the downland. It was also the setting of an intriguing episode when the famous novelist Agatha Christie staged a disappearance here in 1926. Following a furious row with her husband and after she had written to the Deputy Chief*

The Surrey Hills – A Dog Walker's Guide

Constable of Surrey claiming her life was in danger, her car was found near the edge of a chalk pit here. There was no trace of the author despite thousands of people conducting a search on the Downs. A day after her disappearance and under an assumed name she booked into a hotel in Harrogate, yet it took ten days before the police caught up with her. The reason for the incident has always remained a mystery. Keep to the right of the gravel path and follow the green waymarker down the hill. At the bottom, turn right and continue along the broad track at the base of Albury Downs. At the far end, bear left where the paths merge and, a few yards further, turn left following the yellow public footpath waymarker. Continue down through the woods, cross the lane and walk up the steps on the other side.

2 Follow the path adjacent to the lane to the far end. At the end when you are facing a cottage turn right along the bridleway.

3 At the far end of the bridleway, having passed the remains of **Tyting Farm**, turn left onto **Halfpenny Lane**. Continue up the lane for a few yards; take the next footpath on the left and start climbing. Where there is a divide in the paths and the path on the right is next to the crest of a bank, keep left. A short distance later there will be a yellow footpath waymarker pointing left: ignore this. Keep going ahead and, a few yards further, keep to the path, which now veers to the left. Continue along this path as it climbs up the hill bearing left where the **North Downs Way** joins from the right. Carry on to the very top of the hill where you will emerge from the woods at **St Martha's Church**.

4 *There is a traditional belief that the original name of the hill was Saints and Martyrs Hill, the martyr being the murdered St Thomas Becket of Canterbury. The Pilgrims'*

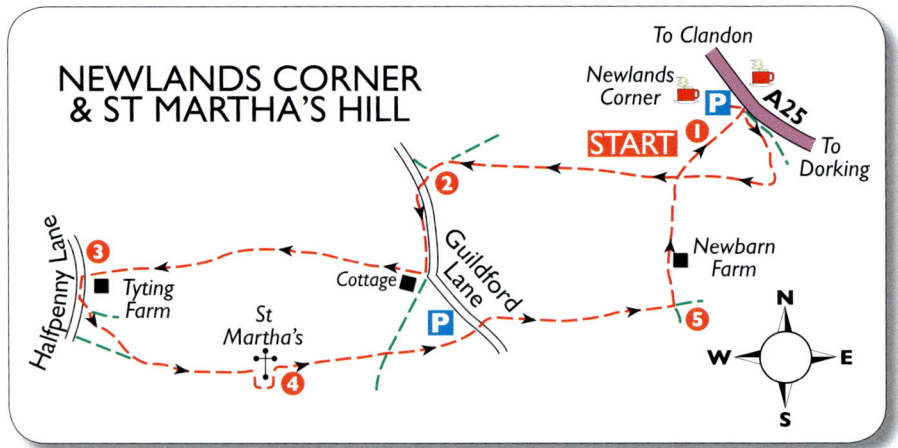

Newlands Corner & St Martha's Hill

Way, which passes the church, was the traditional route for travellers on their way from Winchester to Canterbury to visit his shrine. Turn right around the side of the church. There are some benches to rest and take in the marvellous view. Continue around the churchyard. When you are on the far side of the church, follow the broad sandy path down the hill. Where the signpost for the **North Downs Way** diverges left, keep ahead and, a few yards later, follow the purple waymarker. On the left-hand side, you will pass a Second World War pillbox. Where the paths split three ways take the middle path again following the purple waymarker. Pass the car park on the left and follow the purple waymarker along the path and out into **Guildford Lane**. Cross the road and take the path opposite.

5 At the next crossroads, turn sharp left and leave **Newbarn farm** on your right. When you come to the farmyard opposite a large concrete barn, bear left and take the footpath up the hill. Keep going uphill passing through the treeline and following the path, which veers right up to the very top, bringing you back to the starting point.

St Martha's Church built in the 12th century.

Holmbury Hill

The view from Holmbury Hill looking towards Leith Hill House and Ockley.

This walk takes you from the village of Holmbury St Mary up to the summit of Holmbury Hill through Hurtwood. There is a viewpoint at the top, which is one of the best spots in the Surrey Hills. It lacks the crowds of Box Hill (you have to walk here) and the views are more panoramic than the slightly taller Leith Hill (where you can see north and south, but not east and west through the trees). On a clear day, you can spot the sea in one direction and the towers at Canary Wharf in the other. You will walk mostly through the Hurtwood, which was one of the first estates in England to offer the public a 'right to roam' with 'open access for air and exercise'.

Terrain

A few hundred yards of walking along a quiet lane to start, but otherwise through woods and along mostly broad tracks with easy gradients. After the viewpoint, the path becomes narrower and undulating for a short while, but

Holmbury Hill

evens out in the woods. There is a final steeper gradient down to the village green at the end of the walk.

Where to park
Park at the village green at Holmbury St Mary (GR TQ 109445). Alternatively park in the Royal Oak pub car park if you visit the pub, but confirm at the bar.

How to get there
Sat Nav RH5 6PG. At Abinger Hammer village on the A25 Guildford Road, follow the sign for Holmbury St Mary. It will be on your right if coming from Guildford and left from Dorking. Holmbury St Mary is a couple of miles down the road, with the village green being on the right-hand side.
OS map: Explorer 146 Dorking, Box Hill & Reigate.

Nearest refreshments
The Royal Oak (☎ 01306 898010) is right on the village green and is one of our favourite pubs in the Surrey Hills. Refurbished in 2016 by the Time Well Spent chain, it is dog friendly throughout. For more information, visit http://royaloak.timewellspent.co.uk/.

Dog factors
Distance: 2.5 miles / 4 km.
Road walking: An initial distance along a very quiet lane.
Livestock: None.
Stiles: None.
Nearest vets: Brelades Vets, Station Road, Gomshall, Surrey, GU5 9LE. ☎ 01483 205 066.

The Walk

1 From the village green at Holmbury St Mary, walk up **Felday Glade**, passing the **Royal Oak** on the left. Walk up the road until it ends at the village hall, then take the track into the woods going in the same direction.

2 Where the paths diverge beneath some telegraph wires, keep right. A few yards later you emerge into a clearing which forms the intersection of five paths. Continue straight ahead (to the right of the metal bench). Carry on straight ahead until you emerge by a pond at the far side of the hill.

The Surrey Hills – A Dog Walker's Guide

❸ *There are some new seats to admire the view. The bench arrangement, named Converse, is one of a series of artworks by local artists commissioned by Surrey Hills Arts. Having walked three quarters of the way around the pond, continue along the footpath, keeping the edge of the hill (and the views) on your right. Keep going as the footpath emerges onto a track. Follow it, bearing right with a blue waymarker showing the way. Follow the track all the way up to the*

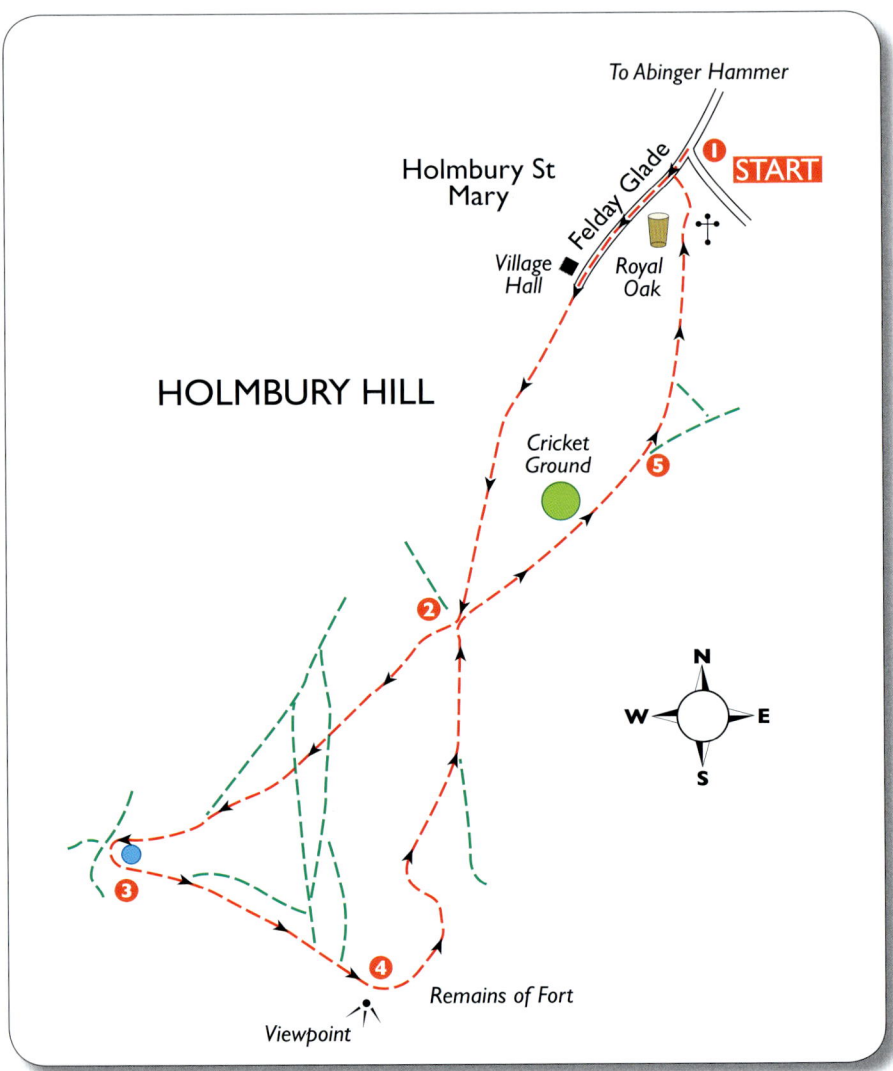

Holmbury Hill

viewpoint. *Holmbury Hill is the fourth highest point in Surrey and home to the ramparts of an Iron Age hillfort.*

4 Having taken time to rest and admire the view, carry on along the footpath in the same direction through the gorse. It will rise and fall, and twist and turn, as you briefly follow the ramparts of the fort. This is the Greensand Way long-distance footpath, so you can follow the yellow waymarkers as the path drops into the woods and becomes a broader track. Follow it back to point 2.

2 **Back at point 2** now turn sharp right, still following the yellow waymarkers. After you pass the cricket ground, there is another divergence.

5 The yellow waymarker points down a wider track dropping to the right. You need to take the left turn. This is still a public footpath and about 100 yards later it crosses a football pitch. Cross the pitch and on the other side the path drops steadily down through some woods (the waymarker post was on the ground on our last visit). Where the path emerges onto a lane, turn right and you will be back on the village green.

Holmbury St Mary is essentially a Victorian village. The village church, which you have just passed on your right, was built as recently as 1873. Although little remains apart from a few concrete foundations, there was an internment camp above the village for both civilian and military prisoners during the First World War.

The vista from the summit of Holmbury Hill.

Leith Hill

At the summit of the hill, Leith Hill Tower stands amongst the woodland.

This is a classic Surrey Hills walk through woodland owned by the National Trust, which takes you to the most famous building in the area: Leith Hill Tower. The tower sits on the second highest hilltop in the south-east and its top is higher above sea level than the Shard in London. On a clear day, you can see sweeping views across 14 counties, from the built-up centre of London to the English Channel.

Terrain
Well signposted footpaths and tracks, mostly through woodland. Although the paths are well used, they can still get muddy in winter, especially on the long, but gentle climb to the tower.

Where to park
Park at the National Trust car park at Rhododendron Wood, just off Tanhurst Lane (charges apply for non-members) (GR TQ 131427).

Leith Hill (10)

How to get there
Sat Nav RH5 6LU. From the M25, exit at junction 9 and continue along the A24 towards Dorking and then towards Beare Green. Then, exit onto the A29, following the signs to Ockley. Go past the pub on the left and turn right, following the signs for Cranleigh/Ewhurst. Proceed along here for about a mile and turn right on the B2126. Take the road signposted to Leith Hill. Proceed up the hill for a mile past Leith Hill Place on the left and take the next turning on the left, Tanhurst Lane. The car park is on the left. **OS map:** Explorer 146 Dorking, Box Hill & Reigate.

Nearest refreshments
There is a servery at the basement of the tower with water bowls for dogs. There are plenty of benches to perch on and enjoy the views with a tea or coffee.

The nearest pub is the Plough Inn at Coldharbour (☎ 01306 711793). Dogs are welcome everywhere apart from the dining room. If you are eating and have your dog with you, the tables in the bar area are ideal. The pub also has the attraction of its own in-house microbrewery. To get there, turn right out of Rhododendron Wood car park, then straight over at the crossroads. Follow the road for one and a half miles and bear left at the end. The pub is on the right-hand side. For more information, visit www.ploughinn.com.

Dog factors
Distance: 2.5 miles / 4 km.
Road walking: A few yards.
Livestock: None.
Stiles: None.
Nearest vets: Brelades Veterinary Surgeons, 20 Knoll Road, Dorking, Surrey, RH4 3EP. ☎ 01306 883086.

The Walk

1 Turn right out of the car park into **Tanhurst Lane**. After a few yards, follow the orange waymarker, turning left up a few steps and then across the road. Follow the path straight ahead on the other side, then bear up the hill.

2 Follow the orange waymarker as the path swings right and continue up through the woods. When you come to a track coming in from your left,

The Surrey Hills – A Dog Walker's Guide

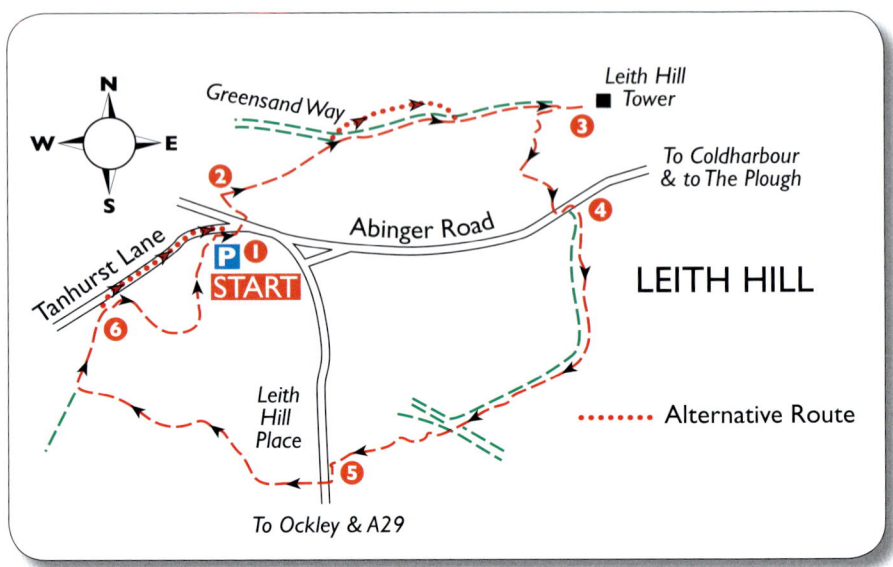

either keep ahead along it or follow the waymarked trail on the left (you will come out at the same place). Now keep ahead until you emerge from the woods and arrive at Leith Hill Tower. *This 18th-century Gothic tower was built around 1765 by Richard Hull of nearby Leith Hill Place. When he died in 1772, at his request he was buried under the tower. The building then fell into ruin and was filled with rubble and concrete, and the entrance bricked up. In 1864 it was reopened, but the concrete made this difficult, and so the additional turreted side-tower was added to allow access to the top. The tower was fully restored by the National Trust in 1984. For a small charge you can climb to the top and take in the detail of the view using a free telescope.*

❸ Retrace your steps a few yards and turn left at the signboard marked with **Woodland Walk** and **Etherley Farm Loop** with an orange arrow. Follow this path right down to the car park (it's about a quarter of a mile down some steep steps).

❹ At the road, turn left, then right, following the orange waymarkers. Follow this broad track as it drops down through the woods. After about half a mile, take the second left ahead at the junction of paths, again following the waymarkers.

❺ At the road turn left and then right a few yards further down at the National Trust sign. Follow the broad grassy path with **Leith Hill Place** to the right.

Leith Hill 10

The Plough in the hamlet of Coldharbour.

Originally dating from the 17th century, Leith Hill Place was refaced in a Palladian style around 1760. The house was opened to the public by the National Trust in 2013 and visitors can walk around and view the restoration, which is still in progress. Leaving Leith Hill Place, follow the orange waymarkers as the path crosses the fields and enters the woods. At the next junction of paths, bear right uphill. Close to the top of the hill, there is another orange waymarker pointing right.

6 You can follow the right turn waymarker, or go straight ahead a few yards further and at the end turn right into **Tanhurst Lane** for a shortcut. If you follow the waymarker the route takes you through **Rhododendron Wood** and back to the car park.

Limpsfield Chart

Home Farm and its dovecote between points 3 and 4.

This walk is at the far eastern end of the Surrey Hills. It takes you from the common at Limpsfield Chart (with its extensive network of footpaths and bridleways) through patches of open heathland, large areas of woodland and out into the fields overlooking the North Downs and Kent. This is a gentle part of the Surrey Hills. Although this walk takes you down one side of a hill, back up and down the other side, the gradients are never too harsh.

Limpsfield Chart

Terrain
Tracks and paths through woods and fields, which can get a bit muddy in the winter. There are long, but very steady gradients.

Where to park
National Trust car park at High Chart (no charge at time of writing) (GR TQ 426521).

How to get there
Sat Nav RH8 0SS. Exit the M25 at junction 6. At the roundabout, follow the signs for the A22 to Eastbourne. At the next roundabout, follow the A25 signed Westerham and Oxted. After you have passed through Oxted, take the right-hand turn onto the B269. At Limpsfield Chart, turn left down Moorhouse Road and the car park is on the right-hand side. Don't confuse the car park with a small parking area, also on the right opposite the common.
OS map: Explorer 147 Sevenoaks & Tonbridge.

Nearest refreshments
Right on the common, at point 6 on the walk, stands the Carpenters Arms (☎ 01883 722209), which dates back to the 1800s and serves award-winning real ales and lagers brewed at the Westerham Brewery. The pub is entirely dog friendly. Dogs are welcome at the tables in the bar area. There is an outside patio at the side overlooking the common and a large garden as well. For more information, visit www.carpenterslimpsfield.co.uk. **Postcode RH8 0TG**.

Dog factors
Distance: 2.5 miles / 4 km.
Road walking: There are very short distances of road walking along a couple of lanes at the middle and end of the walk.
Livestock: We found horses grazing in one of the fields, which the path crossed.
Stiles: A few, but all dog friendly.
Nearest vets: Medivet, 1 Barrow Green Rd, Oxted, Surrey, RH8 0RA.
☎ 01883 712206.

The Surrey Hills – A Dog Walker's Guide

The Walk

1 From the High Chart car park, take the path that leads straight into the woods, just to the left of the information board. Another path will merge very soon in from the right. *The High Chart is a large area of woodland owned by the National Trust which has a network of footpaths. 'Chart' is an Old English word for rough ground. There are magnificent beech trees, some around 200 years old.* At the next divergence of paths, bear left and follow the yellow waymarker.

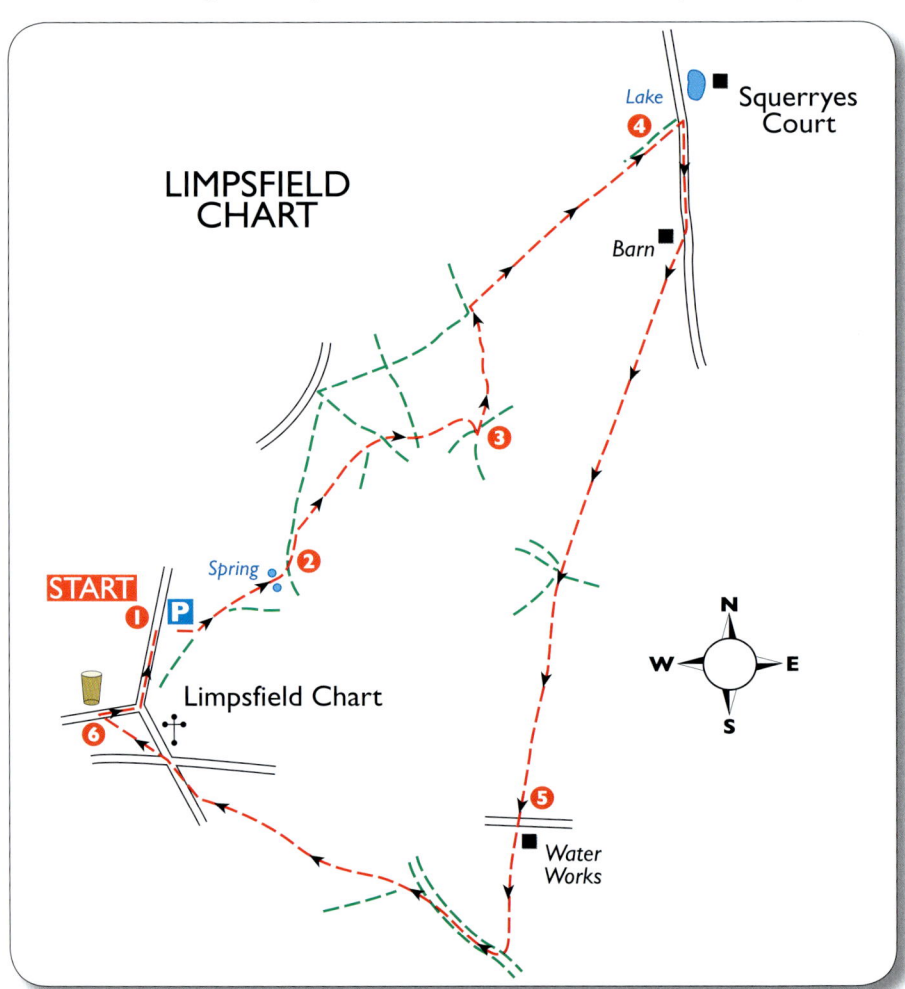

Limpsfield Chart 11

Keep following the yellow waymarkers. The path will drop down through the woods and cross a shallow pond on a low bridge.

② After the bridge, just past the **Titsey Foundation** signpost, bear slightly left and ahead. Follow this track as it makes its way through the woods and clearings.

③ When it comes to an end, you need to take a dog-leg left. Walk a few yards further until you are almost next to the open field and then bear left. You need to be walking along the path downhill with the open field now a few feet away from you through the trees on your right. Where the path dips and just before it rises again there is a crossroads. Turn right, following the yellow waymarker and cross the stile into the field. Continue through the field with

Heading through the woods at Limpsfield Chart.

The Surrey Hills – A Dog Walker's Guide

the hedge line immediately to your left. *The Dovecote on the hillside was built in the 18th century and is a listed building, although it has not been used to house birds since the First World War.* Carry on over the next stile and continue in the next field. About half way along, the path passes through the hedge line. Turn right along the tarmac drive to the end.

4 At the end of the drive, turn right up the lane for a very short distance, taking the footpath on the right just after the barn. As you walk up the lane, take a glance over your right shoulder to see the folly on top of the hill. You now keep ahead, gently uphill through the field and up into the woods. At an intersection of five tracks, keep ahead. At the far end, you will cross a road.

5 Keep ahead with the waterworks on the left and follow the path where it drops steeply down the other side of the hill and emerges onto a tarmac drive. Turn right along the drive. A short distance later, take the path that diverges left, following the **Tandridge Border Path** waymarker. Continue along this path, but at the next divergence keep ahead and do not drop further down the hill. Follow the path all the way gently up the hill. Where it emerges onto a drive, bear right and you will soon find yourself facing **Limpsfield Chart Common**. Continue in the same direction over the road and take the path that crosses the common.

6 At the other side you will be facing the **Carpenters Arms** pub. Outside the pub, turn right and at the end of the road turn left. The car park is a short distance further down on the right-hand side.

Loseley Park

Looking towards the North Downs after point 7 on the walk.

This walk takes you through classic Surrey Hills territory. En route, you'll find an ancient country pub, an imposing Tudor manor house and the Arts and Crafts gem that is Watts Gallery – Artists' Village. As you walk though fields and woods in the shadow of the North Downs you'll be treated to a dose of culture, as well as history.

Terrain
Quiet country lanes, footpaths and broad tracks. At one point, you will follow the North Downs Way long-distance footpath. There is one steady uphill climb.

The Surrey Hills – A Dog Walker's Guide

Where to park
There is space for a few cars off Polsted Lane, Compton (GR SU 963469), or very close by at the Withies Inn on Withies Lane.

How to get there
Sat Nav GU3 1JD or **GU3 1JA.** From the A3, take the B3000 exit for Compton. After the village green, turn left along Polsted Lane. There are some parking spaces on the left. Don't go beyond the dead-end sign. In front of the sign, turn sharp right and the Withies Inn is a short distance down the lane. **OS map:** Explorer 145 Guildford & Farnham.

Nearest refreshments
There is a tea shop in the Watts Gallery – Artists' Village at point 6 on the walk. Dogs are allowed at the tables outside. There is no table service on the benches on the gravel – choose those nearer the building.

The Withies Inn (☎ 01483 421158) is an ancient 16th-century country pub. Dogs are not allowed inside, but they are allowed in the gardens where some of the tables have been incorporated into a hedged pergola to create an unusual outside dining experience. Water bowls are provided for the dogs. For more information, visit www.thewithiesinn.com.

Dog factors
Distance: 4 miles / 6.4 km.
Road walking: An initial distance along an extremely quiet lane and a later short distance again along a quiet lane.
Livestock: None.
Stiles: All dog friendly.
Nearest vets: Farncombe Veterinary Surgery, 24 St Johns Street, Farncombe, Surrey, GU7 3EJ. ☎ 01483 421833.

The Walk

1 Walk ahead from the parking places in **Polsted Lane**, or alternatively walk up the lane from the pub. Follow the lane to the very end.

2 Turn right along the track. Continue until a gate blocks the path with the footpath sign pointing left. Follow the path, which will soon turn right again.

Loseley Park (12)

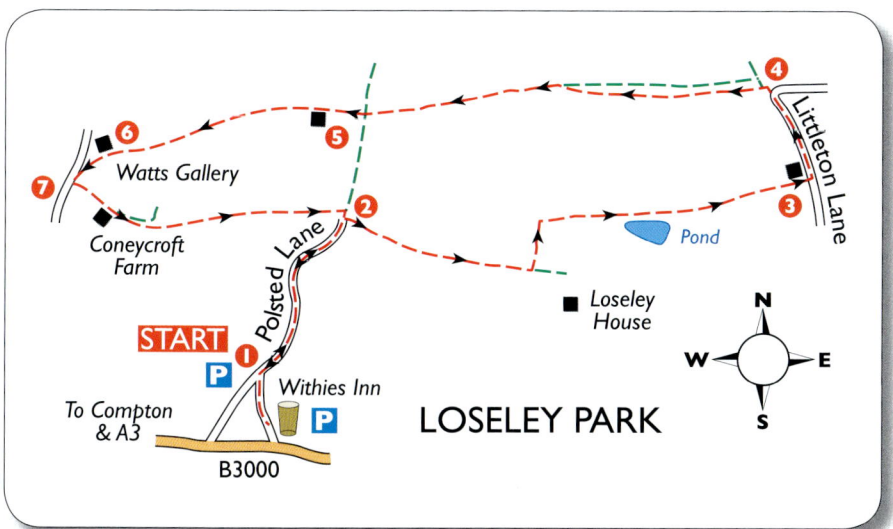

Cross the stile with views of Loseley House to your right. *The house was built between 1562 and 1568, and it is claimed that the new house replaced a smaller one which Elizabeth I had declared inadequate for her to visit. The house has remained in the same family for 500 years.* Go through the gate on your right and continue in the same direction, keeping the pond to your right and past the benches. Keep ahead through the next gate and cross the next field. Go through the gate next to the house.

❸ When you come out onto the lane, turn left and walk up the hill.

❹ At the top, keep ahead when the lane turns right. A few yards further on, take the path on the left. Now, just keep going through the woods. At a crossroads of paths, keep ahead.

❺ Passing a farm on the left, continue along the track in the same direction.

❻ Once the track drops downhill, you will have a view of the **Watts Gallery** on the right. Entry to the site is at the end of the track, not through the gate. *Founded in 1904, Watts Gallery and its Artists' Village are dedicated to the life and work of Victorian artist George Frederic Watts who was widely considered to be the greatest painter of the Victorian era. While dogs are not allowed inside the buildings you can certainly soak up some of the atmosphere whilst sitting outside at the tea shop.* Back on the walk, where the track emerges out onto the lane, with the gallery entrance on the right, you need to turn left.

The Surrey Hills – A Dog Walker's Guide

7 Take the next footpath on the left. If you have walked down the lane as far as the chapel you have missed it. The path will soon turn sharp right and immediately left onto a tarmac track. Where this track ends, do not go through the gate immediately facing you. The footpath is on the right and then a couple of yards further on a left turn. Now continue ahead in the same direction. Where the path drops down some steps into a sunken lane, turn right at the bottom. You will be back at point 2. Retrace your steps back to your chosen start point.

The Watts Gallery as seen from the walk.

Polesden Lacey

The magnificent house at Polesden Lacey.

This walks takes a wide circuit around one of the most famous houses in the Surrey Hills. Polesden Lacey is an Edwardian house and estate, now owned by the National Trust. For many years, it was owned by Margaret Greville, a well-known Edwardian socialite. You will be walking along some of the footpaths and tracks that crisscross the estate. The route is undulating, following the contours of the land and you will have some fine views of the house. There is no need to buy an admission ticket to enjoy the walk, but – if you do – you can take a closer look at the house and walk your dog along the garden terrace and through some of the grounds. We have

The Surrey Hills – A Dog Walker's Guide

incorporated a shortcut into the walk if you wish to do this. Polesden Lacey is one of the more dog-friendly National Trust properties and even has its own dog walking club.

Terrain
This route is mostly through woodland. There are a few gradients up and down, but nothing too challenging. At the start and end, there may a little road walking, depending on where you park.

Where to park
Park in the main National Trust car park (charges apply for non-members) (GR TQ 134524). There is a much smaller car park at North Lodge at point 2 on the walk (GR TQ 136527).

How to get there
Sat Nav KT23 4PZ. From junction 9 of the M25, follow the A243 (sign posted A24 Epsom, Dorking and Leatherhead), then take the A24 and then the A246 (follow the brown tourist signs). At Great Bookham, follow the brown sign indicating the left turn to Polesden Lacey. From Guildford, follow the A246, past East Clandon and East Horsley. Then follow the brown tourist sign at Great Bookham that indicates a right turn to Polesden Lacey. **OS map:** Explorer 146 Dorking, Box Hill & Reigate.

Nearest refreshments
The Cowshed Coffee Shop at Polesden Lacey, which you can access without paying the admission fee. It serves the usual National Trust fare and there are plenty of pleasant outside tables.

Dog factors
Distance: 4.5 miles / 7.2 km.
Road walking: An initial distance along the entrance drive to the house.
Livestock: If you keep to the route you will not cross any fields and therefore should not encounter any livestock. However, there are working farms on the estate if you venture further afield.
Stiles: None.
Nearest vets: Brelades Vets, Rothwell House, Church Road, Bookham, Surrey KT23 3JP. ☎ 01372 452 531.

Polesden Lacey 13

The Walk

1 From the main National Trust car park, retrace your steps alongside the entrance drive back through the impressive entrance arch. At the cottage on the other side, turn sharp left past the small **North Lodge car park**.

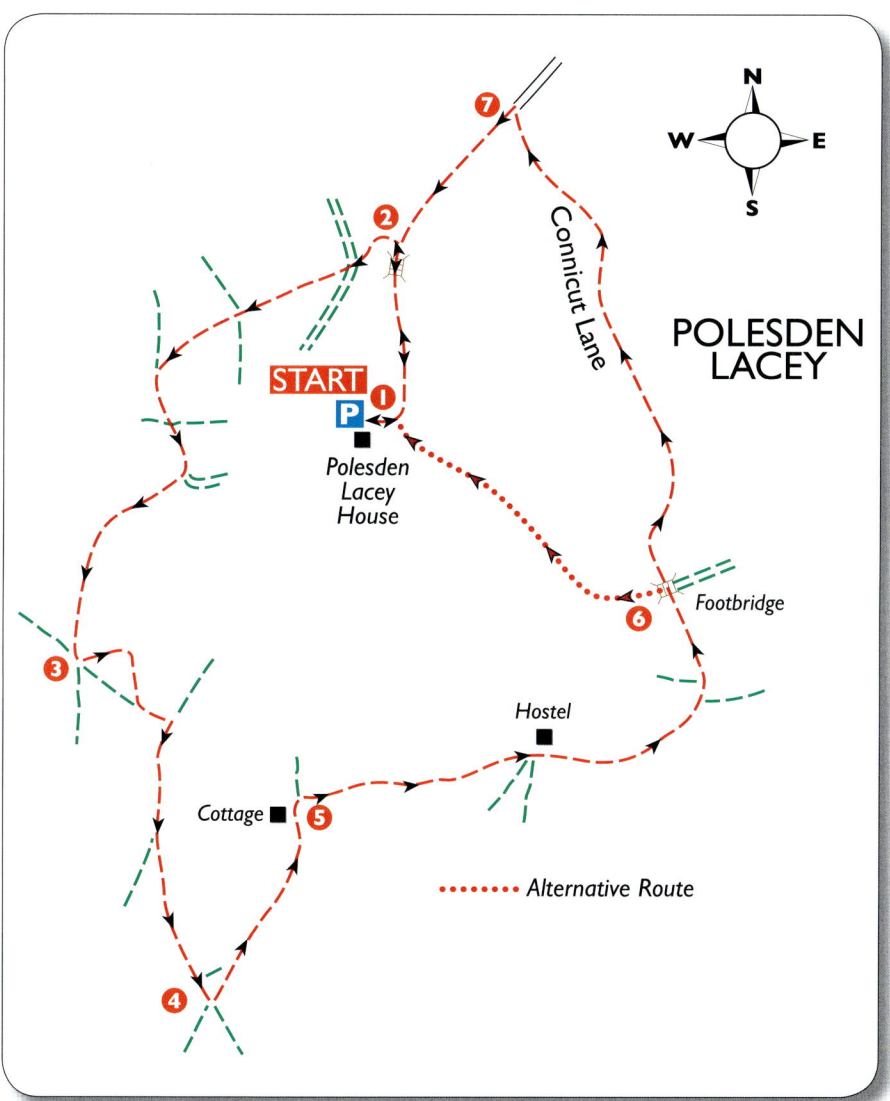

63

The Surrey Hills – A Dog Walker's Guide

Walking through the North Lodge at the start of the walk.

❷ Continuing past the car park, take the middle of the three diverging lanes. Continue up to the woodland. On your right, there are long views back towards London on a clear day. Follow the track as it curves through the woods. Keep ahead at the crossroads. As views of the valley open up on the left, follow the track as it curves to the right and drops downhill.

❸ At the bottom of the hill, take the track that turns to the left. Follow it up the hill and you will emerge opposite **Yew Tree Farm**. Take the track on the right in front of the farm. Continuing on the track, you'll find a bench on the left where you can sit and take in the view of **Polesden Lacey House**. *The first house was built here in the 14th century. In 1824, a new house was designed by famous architect Thomas Cubitt whose work also included the east front of Buckingham Palace and Osborne House on the Isle of Wight. In the early 20th*

Polesden Lacey

century, the new owners employed the architects responsible for London's Ritz Hotel to transform Cubitt's House into a glittering venue suitable for hosting the elite.

4 In the woods, follow the sign directing the National Trust blue and purple walks to the left. You will dog-leg back to the left and follow the track back down through the woods.

5 An isolated cottage will be on your left. Immediately afterwards, follow the blue and purple National Trust waymarkers right. Follow the path as it drops down through the woods and back up the other side. Continue ahead and pass the **youth hostel** on your left. Follow the path as it drops down to the bottom of the valley and bears left. Near the top of the hill you will pass beneath an ornate bridge.

6 If you have bought an admission ticket, you can shortcut to the house and grounds here. Take the steps on the right under the arch and turn right, crossing the bridge at the top. Then follow this path straight ahead into the grounds. You can bear left along the "Long Walk". *This long grass terrace walk dates from 1671 and was extended by the playwright Sheridan in the 19th century.* Alternatively keep ahead up the track for the house and other gardens. If you don't have an admission ticket, continue along the path right to the end.

7 At the end, turn left along the road. The entrance lodge will be on your left.

Ranmore

St Barnabas church.

This simple and straightforward walk will take you along the side of the North Downs with spectacular views for much of the way. For some of the distance, it follows the National Trust's Denbies Hillside walk. Named after John Denby, a 17th-century farmer, the hillside is home to a great variety of plants and animals, including Adonis blue and chalk hill blue butterflies.

Terrain

Footpaths and trackways, all clearly marked. There is a long steady climb to regain the hilltop after you have taken the more leisurely walk down. There

Ranmore 14

may be plenty of livestock grazing on the hillside, so dogs must be kept under close control.

Where to park
Park in the National Trust car park at Ranmore Common Road (charges apply for non-members) (GR TQ142504).

How to get there
Sat Nav RH5 6SR. From the west end of Dorking town centre, take the A25 and then turn right up Station Road. Continue along Station Road where it bears left but then keep immediately ahead where it becomes Ranmore Road. If you end up at the station itself, you have taken a wrong turn. Keep ahead along Ranmore Road as it climbs steeply up the wooded hillside. When you finally emerge onto the common, the car park is on the left-hand side.
OS map: Explorer 146 Dorking, Box Hill & Reigate.

Nearest refreshments
None on the walk, although you are very close to Dorking town centre to get provisions for a picnic. There are picnic tables in Steers Field at the start of the walk. We found the nearby Denbies Wine Estate visitor centre (TQ165515, RH5 6AA) surprisingly dog friendly. For more information, visit www.denbies.co.uk. While dogs understandably are not permitted inside the restaurant, there are outside tables. The Surrey Hills Brewery is also on the estate, at the back of the building. You can tie up your dog at the main door (you will still be able to see him or her through the open entrance), so you can take a peek in and even try a beer.

Dog factors
Distance: 2.5 miles / 4 km.
Road walking: None.
Livestock: There is potential for livestock on the hillside. A long retractable lead might be a good idea for parts of this walk.
Stiles: None.
Nearest vets: Brelades Veterinary Surgeons, 20 Knoll Road, Dorking, Surrey RH4 3EP. ☎ 01306 883086.

The Walk

❶ Go through the gate into **Steers Field** and bear left past the picnic area,

67

The Surrey Hills – A Dog Walker's Guide

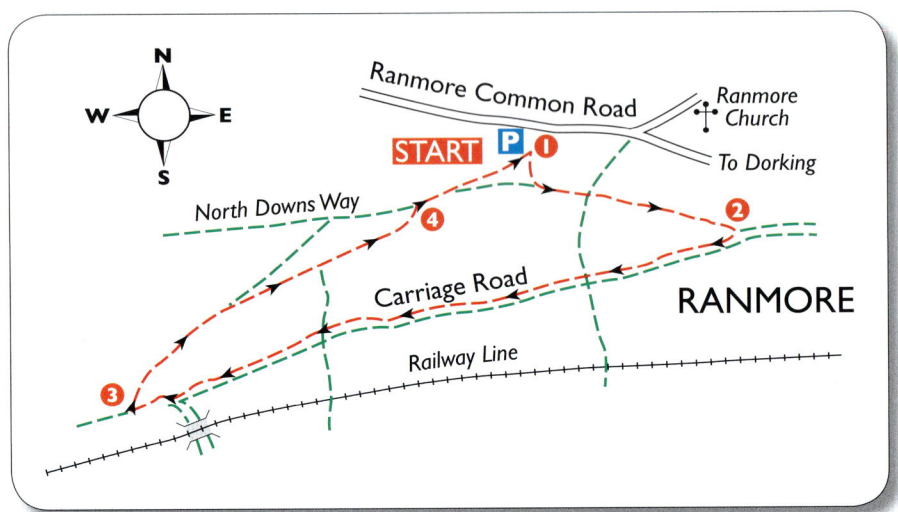

The Surrey Hills landscape along the carriage road.

Ranmore

following the orange waymarked trail as it drops down the side of the hill. Take in the sweeping views, especially to the west across the valley. *To your left is the town of Dorking. Across the valley are the heights of Leith Hill and further west, Holmbury Hill.* Follow the path as it enters the woods and turns sharp right, before dropping down onto the carriage road.

2 At the carriage road turn right. *This track was once the access road for Denbies House, owned by the Ashcombe family.* Follow this track as it gently drops downhill for a mile. When the carriage road emerges onto another track, bear right following the orange waymarker. The path now climbs a little into the woods.

3 A few yards into the woods, turn sharp right, following the orange sign. The path climbs through woods, and then out into the open with views back facing Dorking. Carry on up the hill with the path now entering more woods. Keep ahead along this path, ignoring the National Trust waymarks.

4 At the top, bear right along the signposted **North Downs Way**. When you emerge back into the open you will see the picnic site to your left. Head in this direction, past the benches to the starting point.

You will see the spire of St Barnabas as you come to the end of the walk. If you wish to visit, cross the car park and take the left turn off Ranmore Common Road, which heads into the trees. The church is a Grade II listed building dating from 1859 and remains virtually unchanged. The architect was the famous Sir George Gilbert Scott.

Reigate Fort & Gatton Park

Exploring the remains of Reigate Fort.

This walk takes you along a stretch of hills with downland fields, grasslands, quiet shady woods and some good views. Visit the top of Reigate Hill where the grounds of 19th-century Reigate Fort are dog friendly and free to explore. The fort commands a historic defensive position, looking out over the downs. This walk also takes you through the woodland and grounds of Gatton Park, which were designed by Lancelot 'Capability' Brown, the famous landscape gardener to the aristocracy.

Reigate Fort & Gatton Park (15)

Terrain
Mostly waymarked footpaths and tracks through woods and open country. The walk starts at a high elevation and later drops down with a moderately steep, but steady incline back up. There are a few hundred yards of road walking along the quiet access road to the Gatton Estate.

Where to park
At the car park at the top of Reigate Hill near the junction of the A217 and Wray Lane. At the time of writing, there was no parking charge. It is not a very large car park and fills quickly, so it's best to get there early (GR TQ 262523).

How to get there
Sat Nav RH2 0HX. Exit the M25 at junction 8, following the signs for Reigate. After the roundabout, make sure you are in the left-hand lane of the dual carriageway. Follow the tourist signs for the viewpoint and car park – you will filter off the road quite quickly. Once on Wray Lane, the car park is on the right. **OS map:** Explorer 146 Dorking, Box Hill & Reigate.

Nearest refreshments
At point 1, right at the start of the walk at the car park, the former Reigate Hill Tea Room is now refreshed and rebranded as Junction 8 and has plenty of outside seating. Closing time is dependent on weather.

Dog factors

Distance: 3 miles / 4.8 km.
Road walking: Only a few hundred yards along the entrance drive to Gatton Estate.
Livestock: Follow any seasonal advice that is posted on the information boards.
Stiles: None.
Nearest vets: Priory Veterinary Surgeons, 11 High St, Tadworth, KT20 5SD. ☎ 01737 812496.

The Walk

1 Walk to the far side of the car park, take the path that leads gently uphill to the left of the café and cross the footbridge. *This bridge is claimed to be the*

The Surrey Hills – A Dog Walker's Guide

earliest example of a reinforced concrete footbridge in the country. It was built in 1910 to carry the North Downs Way across the London to Reigate road. Keep following the path in the same direction. After a while it will briefly become a tarmac drive with some houses on the left.

❷ After the houses, turn left into **Reigate Fort**. *Built in the late 19th century, the fort was part of the London Defence Positions, and housed weaponry and equipment. During the Second World War, it was used for billeting Canadian forces. Nowadays, you can walk along the top of the elongated earthwork, which is surrounded by a deep ditch and set on the slope of the North Downs. Inside the fort, you can see the buildings forming the magazine, tool store and two casemates. The entrance to the site is still protected by the original bulletproof gates.* Once you've explored the fort, **return to point 1**.

❶ Continue across the car park and cross the road on the other side. Take the path into the woods. As it curves to the right, take the left-hand turn. Continue as the path goes through the woods and starts to drop downhill. Keep ahead where another path joins from the right. Follow the path to the very bottom of the hill. There will be a cottage on your left, as you emerge onto a quiet lane.

❸ Turn right along the lane (this is the entrance drive to **Gatton Park**) and carry on through the gates until you have the **Millennium Stones** on your right.

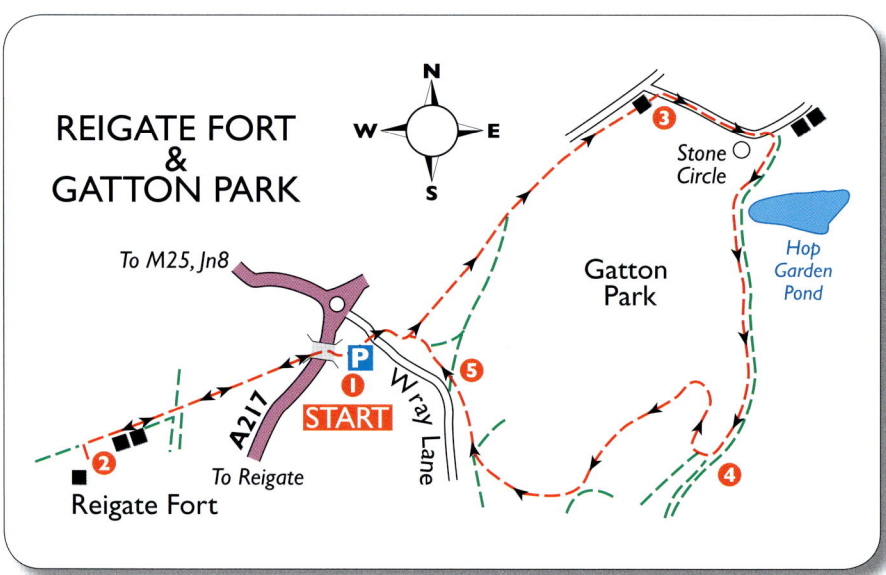

Reigate Fort & Gatton Park (15)

This modern stone circle was originally commissioned as a touring exhibition to mark the new millennium. Ten standing Caithness stones were carved to mark the two millennia from the birth of Christ to the year 2000. The first stone starts with words from St John and the final stone has an extract from poet TS Eliot. Once you have passed the circle take a dog-leg right and follow the track passing the pond on your left. *To the right are views of the landscaped parkland, created between 1762 and 1768 by renowned landscape architect Lancelot 'Capability' Brown.* Continue uphill on the track with some fine views on your left.

4 Where the paths diverge and you have the high fence to your left and some buildings facing you, take the right-hand path through the black gate. Follow the orange **North Downs Ridge** waymarker. Then, immediately turn sharp right following the **Discover Gatton** metal waymarker. Take this path as it climbs up and around into the woods. When you reach a rough crossroads of tracks with a metal bench, bear right. Continue on this track and when you get to the next rough crossroads, keep ahead through the gate. You will emerge from the woods and climb the side of the hill with views of **Gatton Park** on your right.

5 When you enter the tree line again, there is another rough crossroads of tracks. Bear right and then immediately left, taking the narrower and steeper path uphill. After a short while you will be back at point 1.

The Millenium Stones at Gatton Park.

Shamley Green & Rowly

The picturesque village green at Shamley Green.

Shamley Green is a quintessentially English village; its triangular green is complete with cricket pitch and lined with dainty cottages and a village pub. The walk takes you through fields and riverside meadows, and features two abandoned forms of transportation: the lost Wey and Arun Canal, and the former Horsham to Guildford railway line, which now forms the Downs Link path.

Terrain
Apart from an initial 80-yard stretch, the entire walk is along designated footpaths and bridleways. It's mostly flat walking in the valley of the River Lox.

Shamley Green & Rowly

Where to park
There is plenty of unrestricted parking around the village green (GR TQ 031438).

How to get there
Sat Nav GU5 0UB. From Guildford, take the A248 through Shalford and then the B2128 through Wonersh. Shamley Green is about half a mile further on. From the south, take the A281. At Bramley, take the right turn for Wonersh.
OS map: Explorer 145 Guildford & Farnham.

Nearest refreshments
Facing the village green at the start of the walk is the Red Lion (☎ 01483 892202), which welcomes dogs on leads in the bar area. For more information, visit www.redlionshamleygreen.co.uk.

The Bricklayers Arms (☎ 01483 898377) is slightly further up the hill between points 1 and 2. For more information, visit www.bricklayersarmspub.co.uk.

Dog factors
Distance: 5 miles / 8 km, or 8 miles / 12.8 km for the extended version.
Road walking: An initial short distance.
Livestock: None.
Stiles: 6, but no dog impediments.
Nearest vets: Oak Barn Vets, Tilehouse Barn, Tilehouse Farm Offices, East Shalford Lane, Guildford, GU4 8AE. ☎ 01483 455355.

The Walk

1 Turn right past the post office and keep to the path on the right of the wide verge. Where this narrows, keep on the pavement past the **Blacksmiths Arms** and cross the road to use the pavement on the other side. Where this ends, there will be 80 yards of road walking adjacent to the church. Take great care as this road can be busy at times.

2 Cross the road again as if to go into the church's car park, but take the footpath on the left in front of the entrance, which runs parallel to the road. A short while later, the footpath will bear right across a field. It may be indistinct, but just head towards the brow of the hill. When at the top, the exit is near

The Surrey Hills – A Dog Walker's Guide

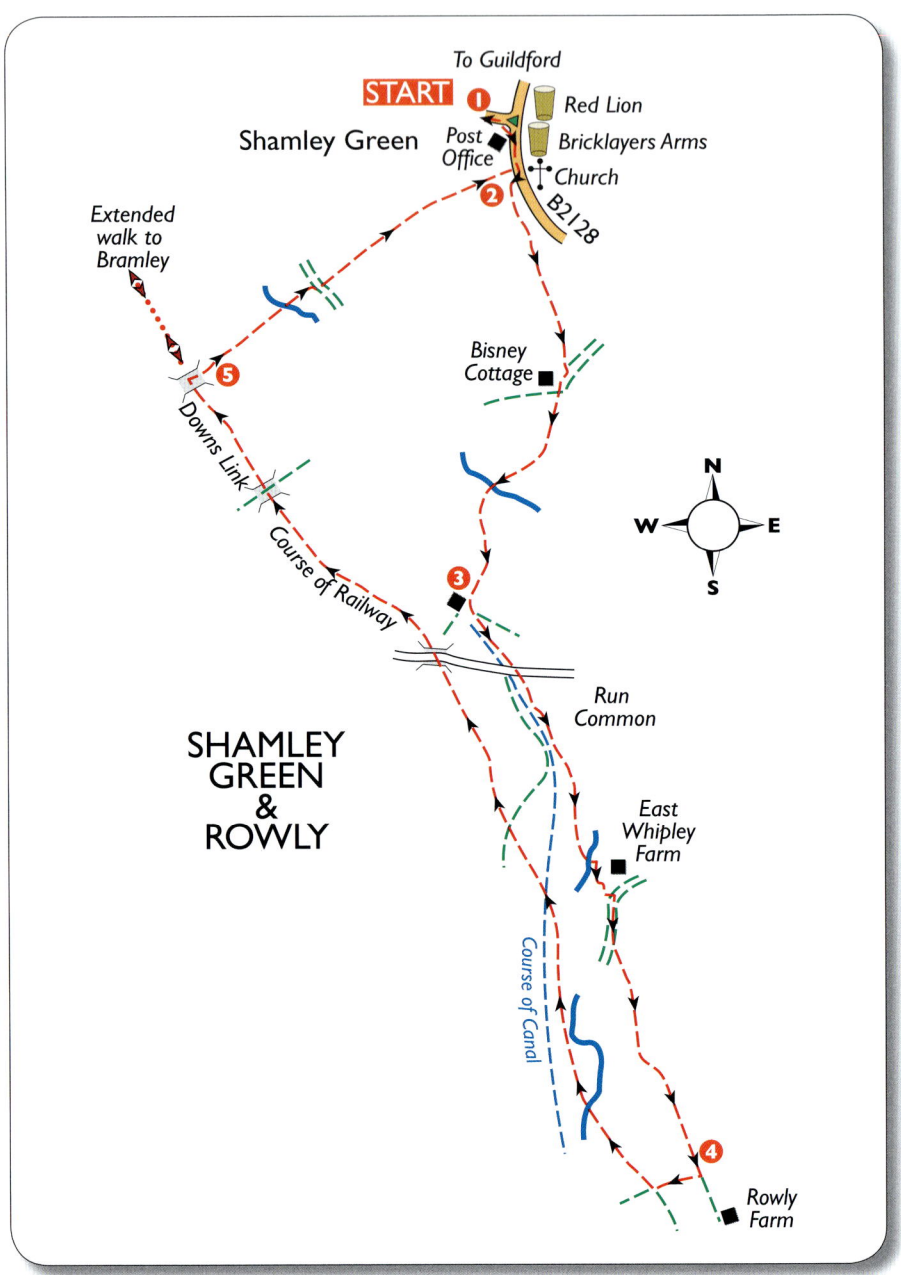

Shamley Green & Rowly (16)

the far corner of the field to the left of the cottages. You then emerge on a tarmac drive and turn right, keeping ahead with **Bisney Cottage** on your right. Follow the path as it drops gently down through pleasant woodland. Continue across the stile then cross the field following the yellow waymarker. After you have crossed the river, continue up the deep sided track, following it as it bears right through the woods.

3. You will emerge facing a driveway and a house. Before you get to the house, turn sharp left, following the footpath sign. Shortly after, bear right off the track along the footpath following the yellow waymarker. You will now be walking along the towpath, with the remains of the canal on your right. When you come to a road, cross it and keep the remains of the canal on the right. After a while, cross the stile as the path veers left away from the canal and follow the path as it crosses a field. At the far end, turn right once you have crossed the river. You will shortly come to a stile and gate. Go through and walk up the path, turning sharp right at the track a few yards later. Continue along the track. Once you have passed the next bridge over the river, take the left-hand fork where the track divides then immediately swing right following the yellow waymarker. The path will now be following the course of the power lines. Continue ahead as the path twists and turns. Once you have passed the end of the field boundary with the woods on the left, continue across the open fields.

The restored platform at Bramley & Wonersh station.

The Surrey Hills – A Dog Walker's Guide

4 Take the next turn on the right. If you have continued as far as **Rowly Farm**, you will have gone too far and will need to turn back. Follow this path as it drops gently downhill between the fields. Once you have crossed the stile at the tree line, turn sharp right, following the **Downs Link** waymarker. *You are now walking along the trackbed of the old railway line, which was originally part of the Horsham to Guildford railway that opened in 1865 and closed about a hundred years later. The line was never very profitable and the 1963 'Reshaping of British Railways', also known as the Beeching report, stated it was used by less than 5,000 passengers per week. The axe duly swung and it closed in 1965, just four months before its 100th anniversary. The footpath was opened in 1984 creating a walking link between the North and South Downs Way. There has been a full feasibility study for reopening the railway and although the proposal was found to be uneconomic, the route is now protected in case circumstances change and it is viable for the trains to one day return.* Take notice of the bridges under which you are walking, as you will need to count them in order to leave the trackbed at the right place. You may also notice that a couple of the bridges still have the remains of the old railway telegraph poles attached.

5 You need to leave the old railway line at the third bridge. Once you have passed beneath the arch turn sharp left and up the side of the cutting. At the top of the steps turn left into the lane. After a short distance, keep ahead following the yellow waymarker. At this point you have just crossed the course of the canal, which has completely vanished into the landscape. Continue along the path, cross the river and, when you emerge onto a tarmac drive, turn right and then immediately left. Keep following the path as it climbs gently out of the valley and, at the top, you will be back at point 2.

If you want to either make it a longer day out, or see some more of the old railway's past, don't turn off the walk at point 5, instead keep ahead along the **Downs Link** path. A mile later you will come to the remains of **Bramley and Wonersh Station**. *In 2004 the derelict remains of the station underwent major renovation works, undertaken by the local council and the Bramley Historical Society. The overgrown site was cleared, and the platform restored and a replica waiting room and level crossing gates installed. The big signs are original, the enamel one was returned, apparently after being used for many years as a shelf in a greenhouse! All that remains of the demolished station house is the pillar box which had been incorporated into its front corner wall.* Once you have had a look around return back to point 5 and turn left to regain the walk.

Tatsfield

An autumn view at point 2 of the walk.

This ramble takes you through the quiet lanes and footpaths at the far eastern edge of the Surrey Hills where they seamlessly merge with the North Downs of Kent. There is plenty of variety with woodland walks and footpaths, and fine views from the slopes of the hills looking both towards Kent and back into Surrey.

Terrain
A mixed bag of footpaths, bridleways, quiet leafy lanes and a short distance along a busier road. There are a few gradients, but nothing too arduous. There are several stiles, but all can be negotiated by dogs of any size with no signs of any attempts to block or wire any up.

Where to park
Although the larger car park at the site has now been closed and blocked off with bollards, there is a free parking area opposite St Mary's Church in Church Hill (GR TQ 417561).

The Surrey Hills – A Dog Walker's Guide

How to get there
Sat Nav TN16 2JX. Don't worry about seeing postcodes relating to Kentish postal districts – that's just for postal convenience; you won't be leaving the Surrey Hills. Take the A25 through Limpsfield into Westerham. In the town centre, take the left turn along the B2024 signposted for Croydon. At the crossroads, take the right turn, with a brown tourist sign for Park Wood Golf Course. The parking area is at the top of the hill opposite the church.
OS map: Explorer 147 Sevenoaks & Tonbridge.

Nearest refreshments
Ye Old Ship (☎ 01959 577311) in Tatsfield village. Continue past the church, turn left at the crossroads and follow the lane. The pub is on the right as you come to the village green. You know your dog will get a suitable welcome when you see the large paw sign on the front door. There are comfy chairs at the front of the pub, where you can sit with your dog, and a large garden at the back. The beers are good too, with a range including a local Surrey-brewed house beer by Croydon's The Cronx Brewery. **Postcode TN16 2AG**.

Dog factors
Distance: 2.5 miles / 4 km.
Road walking: Short distances, firstly along a very quiet lane and later a short section on a busier road where you will need your dog on a lead and under close control.
Livestock: Horses were grazing in the field after point 5.
Stiles: Several, but none with any problems.
Nearest vets: Darwin Veterinary Centre, 2 Haig Road, Biggin Hill, Kent, TN16 3LJ. ☎ 01959 541153.

The Walk

1 Take the footpath from the parking area on the opposite side of the road from the church. Do not go onto the golf course. Follow the path as it bears right and heads downhill through an area of dense trees. At the bottom turn left along **Chestnut Avenue**.

2 Continue along the road until you reach the first footpath on the right. It's quite hidden, but it is underneath a set of telegraph wires. If you have houses on the right in the lane, you have gone too far and need to turn back. Follow

Tatsfield 17

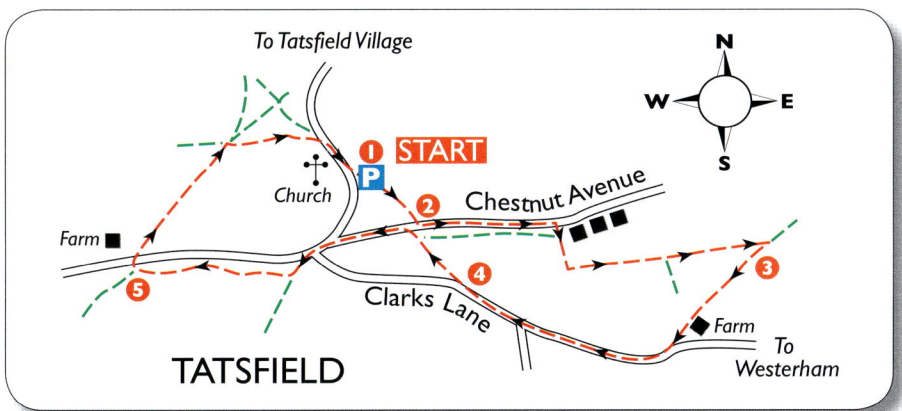

the footpath as it drops down the hill and bear left where another path diverges from the right. A few yards later there will be a staggered crossroads of paths, turn left here. Continue along this path. On the right you'll have views of the hills and the town of **Westerham**. Continue along the path, ignoring the first right turn. Keep ahead following the green self-guided trail waymarker.

3 Take the next dog-leg right where the bridleway drops downhill. At this point, we found the waymarker and gate had been crushed by a fallen tree. Follow the bridleway to the bottom of the hill. Where it emerges onto a road, turn right. There will now be a short distance of road walking.

4 Take the next footpath on the right. This is well hidden, but there is a footpath sign on the left of the road. As the path climbs up through the woods, take the right-hand divergence and follow it all the way up to the road. **You will now be back at point 2**.

2 Now turn left along **Chestnut Avenue**. At the end where you come to a junction of three roads, head to the far left-hand side where there is another footpath sign and take the path that drops down the hill. Where it emerges through a gate into a field, follow the yellow waymarker turning right and take the path next to the treeline on the right. Follow this path through the first field and a gate, and continue until the path curves slightly to the right. There you'll find access back onto the road.

5 Cross the road and go over the stile, taking the footpath to the right of the farm building and access drive. Continue diagonally across the field. Cross

The Surrey Hills – A Dog Walker's Guide

the stile at the end and turn right along the track. Where the track turns left, there is a stile hidden in the hedge on the right. Cross the stile and turn immediately right in the lane. A very short distance later, you'll be back at the start. Before you drive off, take some time to have a look at **St Mary's Church**. The churchyard offers fine views across the Surrey Hills.

An evening view across the hills at point 5 on the walk.

Titsey

Titsey Place as seen from one of the viewpoints.

This walk explores one of the lesser-known parts of the Surrey Hills. But, thanks to the Titsey Foundation – a charity committed to preserving public access to this part of the hills – there is plenty to see and do. The walk passes Titsey Place, a manor house with Tudor origins, set in beautiful landscaped gardens and parkland.

Terrain

Paths and tracks are mostly through woodland along the side of the North Downs, and through parkland and fields at the bottom of the valley. There is a stiff climb at one point, and an even steeper descent where handrails have been provided on both sides of the path. This walk is not recommended after heavy rain, or when it could be slippery.

The Surrey Hills – A Dog Walker's Guide

Where to park
Botley Hill Car Park off the B269 at the junction with Clarks Lane and Titsey Hill. There is currently no charge (GR TQ 398554).

How to get there
Sat Nav CR6 9QH. Travelling along the A25 between Oxted and Westerham, turn into Limpsfield High Street. At the bottom of the High Street, follow the road as it turns right ignoring the sign to Titsey Place. Continue underneath the motorway, passing the church on the right hand side, and carry on as the road climbs up the hill. The car park is in the trees at the top on the left. **OS map:** Rather annoyingly split between Explorers 146 Dorking, Box Hill & Reigate and 147 Sevenoaks & Tonbridge.

Nearest refreshments
The Titsey Place Tea Room (☎ 01273 715356) at point 3. There are outside benches where you can sit with your dog. For more information, visit www.titsey.org. A few hundred yards from point 1 along the B269, the Botley Hill Farmhouse (☎ 01959 577154) is a 16th-century pub with the Sheep Shed tea room in one of the side buildings. The pub is dog friendly and there are benches and a rear garden where you can eat outside. For more information, visit www.botleyhill-farmhouse.co.uk.

Dog factors
Distance: 4 miles / 6.4 km.
Road walking: A short distance along the entrance drive to the manor house.
Livestock: None.
Stiles: None.
Nearest vets: Darwin Veterinary Centre, 2 Haig Rd, Biggin Hill, Westerham, TN16 3LJ. ☎ 01959 541153.

The Walk

 Turn sharp left out of the car park and on the track that drops downhill through the woods. Although this is called **Pitchfont Lane**, you can see from the barrier at the top that it is closed to traffic. Follow the track as it drops right, eventually passing the farm on the left. After you have passed through a metal gate you will soon see **Pitchfont Lodge** on the left.

Titsey 18

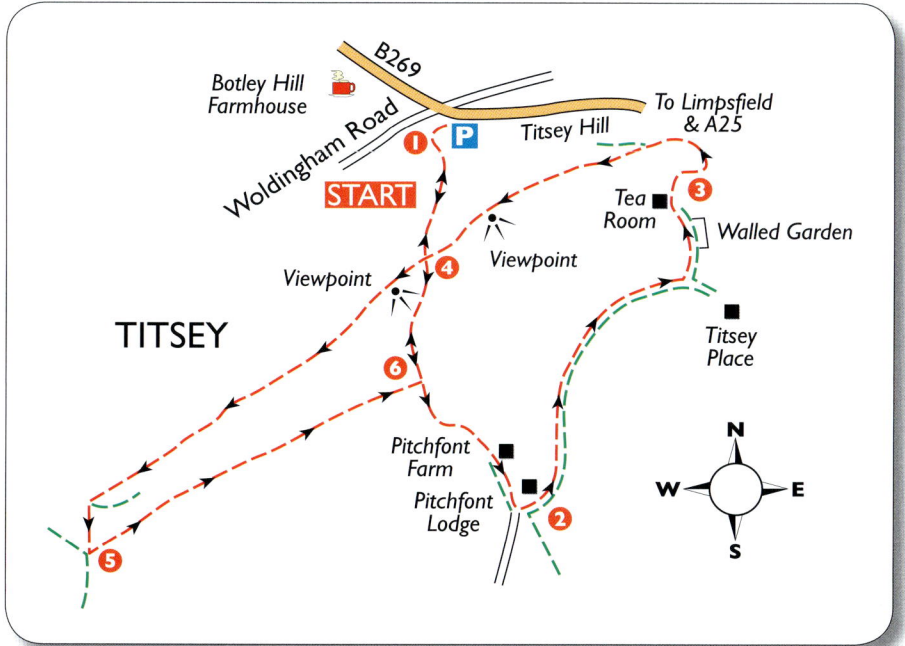

2 At the lodge, turn left through the wooden gates and walk up the drive. You will soon see **Titsey Place** on the right and the church through the trees to its right. Continue up the drive, following it left at the end and passing the walled garden on your right. Bear right behind the tea room, following the Walk sign to the left of the car park.

3 You now take the narrower path heading up the hill with a tall hedge on the right. Follow the path as it twists and turns steeply up the hillside. If in doubt follow the red waymarkers. Once the path has flattened out and there is a divergence, take the lower track. *Most of the walk now takes you through the deeply wooded slopes of the North Downs. This area is known as the Titsey Plantation. It was created between 1807 and 1840 when around half a million trees were planted. In places the trees have been cut back to create some good viewpoints with benches looking back down to Titsey Place and the valley.*

4 When you come to the metal gates, keep going ahead (you will be crossing your outward route here) and follow the red waymarkers. There is a vantage point with a viewing table on the left. When you get to a bench, do not take the dog-left left. Instead follow the red waymarker to the left of the bench taking the very steep path downhill with the wooden handrails on both sides.

85

The Surrey Hills – A Dog Walker's Guide

Follow it to the very bottom and out into the field. *This whole walk takes you through an area managed by the Titsey Foundation, a charitable trust set up in 1979 to manage and preserve Titsey Place. The Titsey Estate covers some 1,800 acres of farm and woodland.*

5 When you have emerged onto the field, keep following the red waymarker and turn sharp left taking the path along the side of the field with the tree line on your left. Follow this path to the end. Go through the gate and down the steps.

6 At the bottom, turn left following the **North Downs Way** sign. You now retrace your steps back up the hill to the start.

The hills at point 5 on the walk.

Waverley Abbey

Inside the remains of the monks' dormitory.

This walk takes you from Tilford, one of the county's traditional villages, to one of the oldest architectural remains in the county – Waverley Abbey, which was England's first Cistercian abbey. Its ruins are situated in a peaceful loop of the River Wey and it's a bit of a hidden gem. In fact, you may find yourself one of only a few visitors, giving you a feel for the solitude of the monks who founded the monastery almost 900 years ago.

Terrain
Mostly footpaths with a couple of short stretches along roads. The walk is mostly level. The whole abbey area is low lying (even in the 13th century it was prone to flooding), so parts of the walk can get quite muddy in winter.

The Surrey Hills – A Dog Walker's Guide

Where to park
There is a small car park facing the river, opposite the Barley Mow pub in Tilford (GR SU 872434). There was no parking fee at the time of writing. There is an alternative car park near the abbey remains, but it is small and a few badly parked vehicles can easily reduce the already limited space.

How to get there
Sat Nav GU10 2BU. Follow the A287 south out of Farnham. In the village of Millbridge, first turn left along The Reeds Road, and then right at the far end. In Tilford, cross the first bridge over the river, then bear left. After the pub on the left, turn sharp right before the road crosses the next bridge. The car park is on the left. **OS map:** Explorer 145 Guildford & Farnham.

Nearest refreshments
At the start of the walk, you'll find the Barley Mow (☎ 01252 792205). Built in the 18th century, it prides itself on being a typical village pub. The pub has a large riverside garden with views over adjoining fields and woodland. It is family-friendly and dogs on leads are welcome. For more information, visit www.thebarleymowtilford.com.

Dog factors
Distance: 3.5 miles / 5.6 km.
Road walking: A couple of short stretches along roads.
Livestock: None.
Stiles: None.
Nearest vets: Elstead Veterinary Surgery, The Green, Elstead, Near Godalming, Surrey, GU8 6DD. ☎ 01252 703412.

The Walk

 Turn right out of the car park and right again, before crossing over the bridge. After the bridge, take the footpath on the left. *Tilford Packhorse Bridge has been described as one of the best-preserved medieval packhorse bridges in England and is a designated Ancient Monument. Two arms of the River Wey converge here and an ancient bridge spans each arm. These were probably built by the monks of Waverley Abbey around the 13th century.* On your left, you will see the remains of Second World War defences. Continue up the path with the valley of the **River Wey** on your left.

Waverley Abbey 19

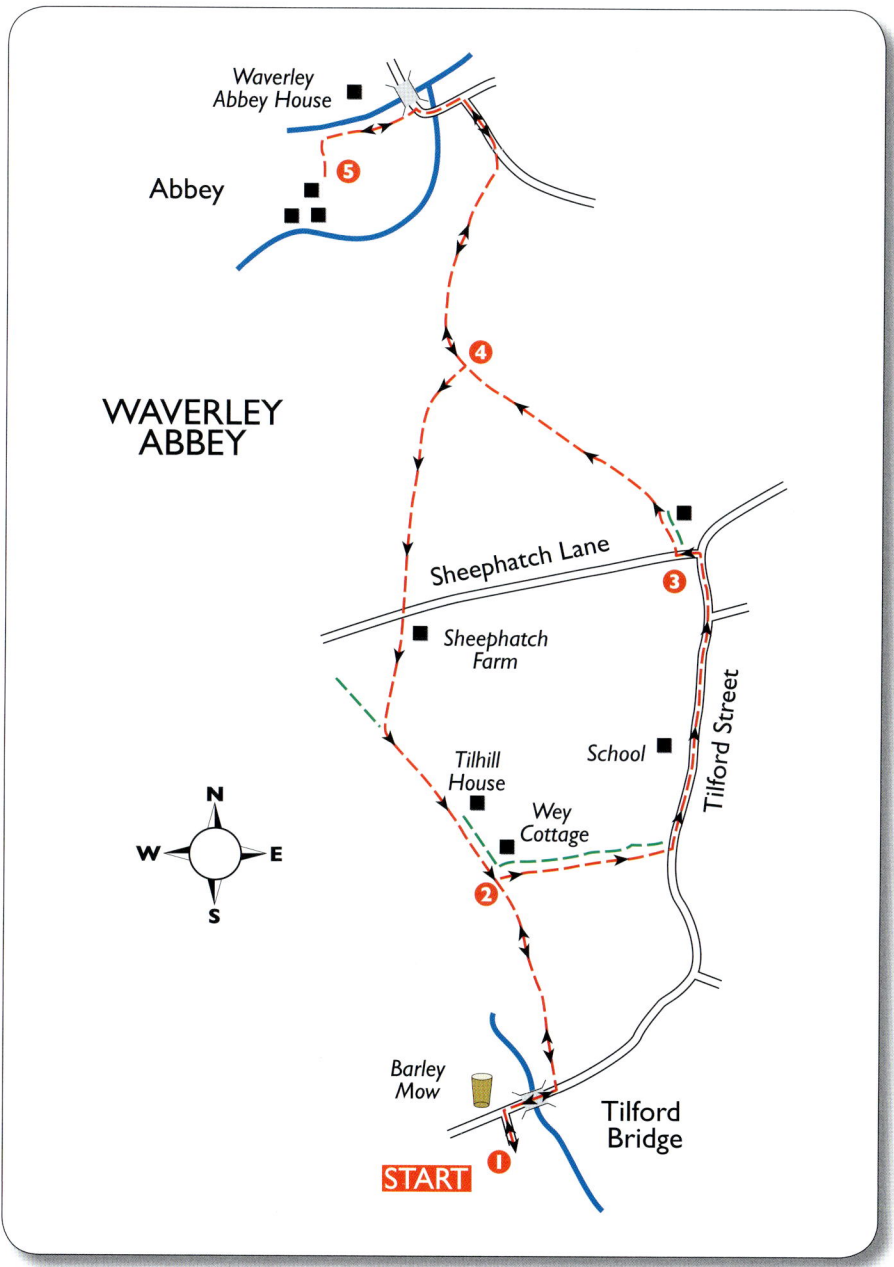

The Surrey Hills – A Dog Walker's Guide

2 When you emerge onto a byway opposite **Wey Cottage**, turn right and follow the byway up the hill to the very end. When you come to the road, turn left. There is a pavement and a grass verge on the left. Keep following the road and turn left into **Sheephatch Lane**.

3 As soon as you have turned into the road, turn immediately right at the public footpath sign and follow the track down through the trees. Once you have passed the houses on the right, keep ahead and go through the gate into the woods.

4 Where a bridleway veers in from the left, keep going ahead and follow the track to the very end, turning left at the road. Once on the road, bear left round the corner at the bottom of the hill past the old mill house on the left and the mill pond on the right. Once you have gone round the corner, turn left following the **Waverley Abbey** sign into the small car park. Here, go through the gate on the far side of the car park on the right and follow the path as it emerges into open fields with an ornamental lake on the right. Across the lake you will have views

The lay brothers' wing on the west side of the site. The upper floor would have been their sleeping quarters, and the lower vaulted area their refectory. In the background is the 18th-century Waverley Abbey House.

Waverley Abbey

of **Waverley Abbey House**. Go through the gate at the end and turn left into the Abbey grounds. *Waverley Abbey was founded in 1128 and was substantially rebuilt during the 13th century. In 1536, with the Dissolution of the Monasteries, the site passed to the treasurer of King Henry VIII's household. Much of the abbey was dismantled and some of the stone was reused to build Loseley House, as well as the new Waverley Abbey House, built in 1723 in the northern portion of the former abbey precinct. Today only parts of the monastic buildings remain and there is little to show of the once great Abbey Church. The most impressive remains are the vaulted undercroft of the lay brothers' refectory where parts of the upper floor and the south wall remain standing. Close by, parts of the monks' dormitory include the full height of the south wall.*

Wagging tails inside the Barley Mow.

5 Once you have explored the Abbey, retrace your steps back to point 4. Here, turn right up the hill following the red public byway arrow. Cross straight over **Sheephatch Lane** with **Sheephatch Farm** on the left. Shortly afterwards bear left again, following the red byway waymarker. Where a field access track crosses the path, keep straight ahead and shortly afterwards bear left where another path joins from the right. You will pass **Tilhill House** on the left. Keep ahead and you will return to point 2 with **Wey Cottage** on your left. Now, bear right down the path you originally came on and return to the start.

Woldingham

The tiny St Agatha's Church.

Less than 30 miles from Central London, this walk takes in hidden valleys, chalk downland and woodlands. The mature woods have a variety of trees including native oak, ash, cherry, beech, whitebeam and field maple. And, in places, coppiced woodland encourages spring flowers and butterflies.

Terrain
Mostly footpaths and tracks with some short distances along quiet lanes or access roads. There is a long but steady climb between points 3 and 5.

Where to park
There is parking at Woldingham station, but high charges apply during the week, as the station is used by commuters. At the time of writing there is parking on the right of the initial stretch of Church Lane.

Woldingham (20)

How to get there
Sat Nav CR3 7JX. Take junction 6 of the M25 and follow the A22 to Croydon. At the next roundabout, take the fifth exit and bear right after passing beneath the railway arch. Woldingham station will be on the right. **OS map:** Explorer 146 Dorking, Box Hill & Reigate.

Nearest refreshments
There's nothing close to the walk; it's a case of bring your own and enjoy the peace and quiet. If you really want to stop somewhere, the Botley Hill Farmhouse pub and tea room (☎ 01959 577154) is only a few miles away. To get there, carry on through Woldingham village along Northdown Road. Turn left into The Ridge and, at the end of the road, take a sharp left turn into Limpsfield Road. The pub and tea room are on the left. For more information, visit www.botleyhill-farmhouse.co.uk. **Postcode CR6 9QH**.

Dog factors
Distance: 3 miles / 4.8 km.
Road walking: Short distances along quiet lanes.
Livestock: None on the walk, but plenty of horses and cattle in adjacent fields who may wish to poke their heads through the fence.
Stiles: None.
Nearest vets: Warlingham Veterinary Centre, 8 The Green, Warlingham, Surrey, CR6 9NA. ☎ 01883 623701.

The Walk

1 Leaving **Woldingham Station**, take a sharp right turn into **Church Lane**.

2 Take the first right, which is signposted **WCW main route**, where the bridge crosses the railway. *Some of this walk is next to the railway line, which was opened in 1884 and includes a mile-long tunnel cut right through the Surrey Hills. From the bridge, you can see the twists and turns designed by the 19th-century engineers for the railway to climb up the valley side to the tunnel. In the background, Woldingham station retains its original wooden Victorian buildings; it is from here that Donald McLean, the infamous spy and local resident, is said to have started his escape and defection to the Soviet Union.* Follow the road as it bears left. Keep ahead, passing **Marden Park Farm** on the right. Once the

The Surrey Hills – A Dog Walker's Guide

access road becomes a broad footpath, keep ahead and enjoy the views of the valley on the right.

3 When you reach a crossroads of tracks with a tall fence on your right, take the left-hand footpath signposted **Woldingham countryside walk** (shortcut). Continue the steady climb up the hill and through the woods.

4 At the left turn signposted **Woldingham station** (main route), keep going ahead and, at the next junction, take the left-hand turn signposted **Great Church Wood and Circular Route** on one side and **Northdown Road** on the other side. If you want to stray off the main route at this point, keep

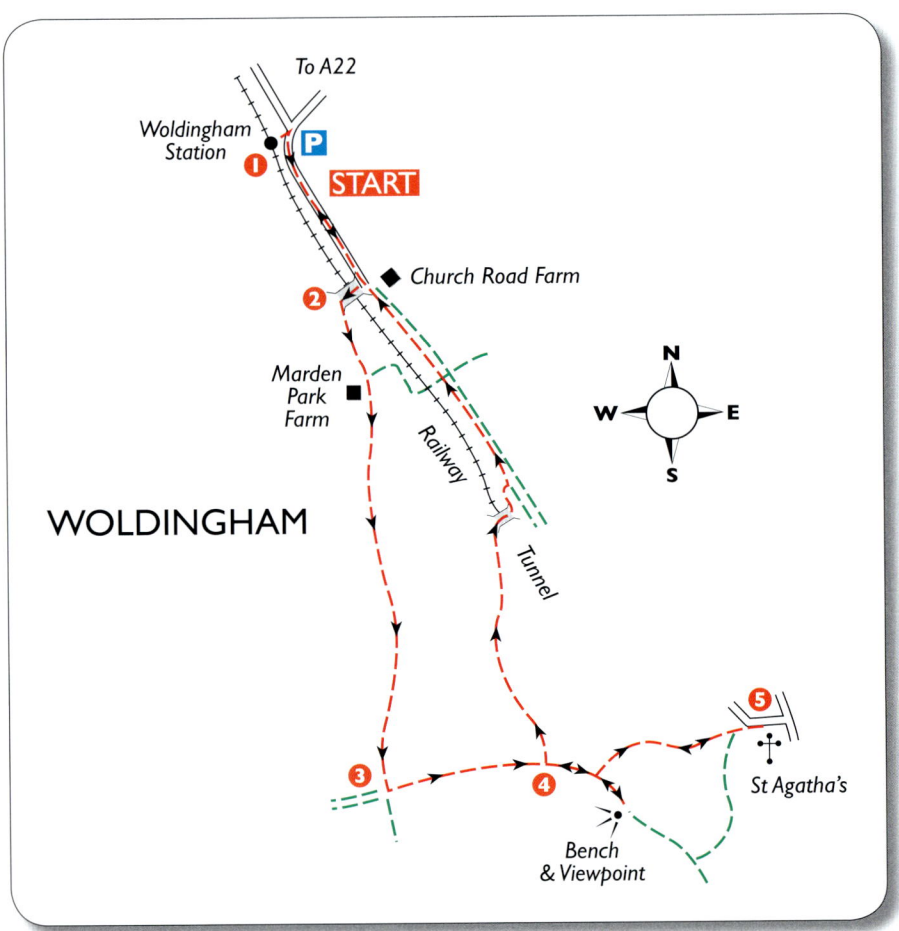

Woldingham

going ahead as a short distance later there is a bench on the left where trees have been cleared to provide a fine view across the valley. Having taken in the view, double back and continue on the main path as it heads up through the woods and curves gently around to the right. On the right, at the top of the hill, there will be an entrance into **Great Church Wood**. Ignore this and continue along the path as it bears left and then immediately right onto a tarmac drive. **St Agatha's Church** is a few yards ahead on the right.

5 *There has been a church on this site since 1291, but the current building, which is claimed to be both the smallest and highest church in Surrey, dates only from 1832. The churchyard contains yew and ash trees (one of the ash trees close to the west door has been dated by Kew Gardens as over 800 years old).* After visiting the church, retrace your steps to point 4. Now follow the sign pointing right to **Woldingham Station** (main route) 1¼ Miles. Continue along this narrower path as it gently drops down through the woods and, at the bottom, take a right turn and follow the yellow waymarker. You are now crossing over the top of the railway tunnel's entrance (there are still chimneys in the woods that were built to vent the smoke from steam locomotives passing through the tunnel). Follow the path left and a few yards further ahead go through the gate on the right and onto **Church Lane**. There, turn left again, following the yellow waymarker. Follow this broad track all the way back to point 1 at the station. Most of the distance is closed to road traffic.

Horses grazing on the slope of the North Downs near the start of the walk.

OTHER TITLES FROM COUNTRYSIDE BOOKS

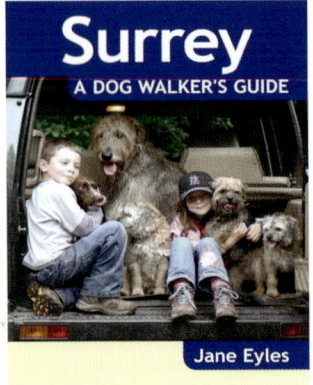
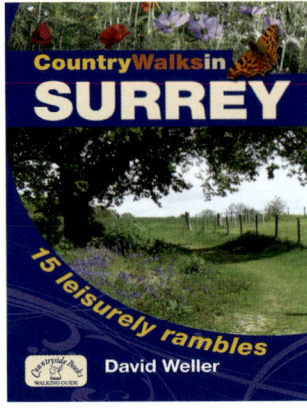
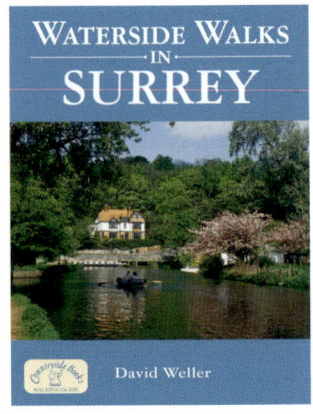

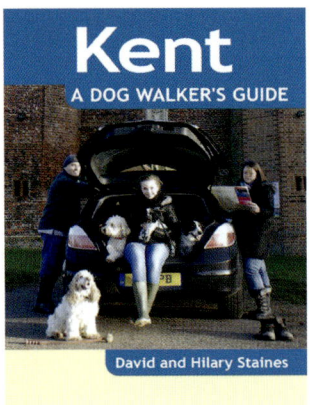
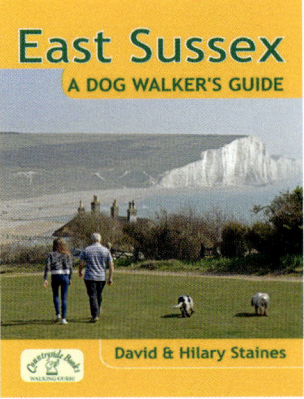
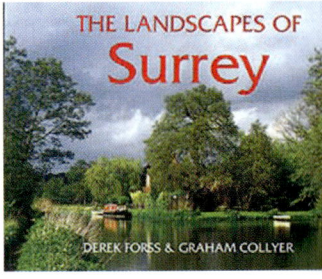

To see the full range of books by Countryside Books then visit
www.countrysidebooks.co.uk
Follow us on @ CountrysideBooks